KINGS, LORDS, & COMMONS

KINGS, LORDS, & COMMONS

An Anthology from the Irish

Irish poems
from the seventh century
to the nineteenth,
translated,
with a
Preface and Introductory Notes
by

FRANK O'CONNOR

FORD & BAILIE, PUBLISHERS
VAN NUYS, CALIFORNIA
1989

Copyright 1959 by Frank O'Connor

This 1989 paperback edition
is published by
Ford & Bailie, Publishers
P.O. Box 2156
Van Nuys, CA 91404-2156

Design by Paula Powers Coe

Library of Congress Cataloging-in-Publication Data
Kings, lords & commons: an anthology from the Irish / translated
by Frank O'Connor.
    p.   cm.
    Reprint. Originally published: New York: Knopf, 1959.
    ISBN 0-926689-00-2
    1. Irish poetry—Translations into English. 2. English poetry—
Translations from Irish. I. O'Connor, Frank, 1903-1966.
    II. Title: Kings, lords, and commons.
PB1424.039 1989
891.6'21008—dc20   89-11756 CIP

Printed and bound in
the United States of America.

Poems in this book (some of them in earlier versions) appeared in two books published by the Cuala Press, Lords and Commons *and* The Wild Bird's Nest; *in* The Fountain of Magic *(Macmillan & Co., Ltd., London, 1939; St. Martin's Press, New York); in* The Midnight Court *(Maurice Fridberg, London, Dublin, 1945); and in* Leinster, Munster and Connaught *(Robert Hale, Ltd., London). Others appeared, often in different form, in Irish and American periodicals. Still others are published here for the first time.*

Preface

This book consists of poems from four smaller books: *The Wild Bird's Nest, Lords and Commons, The Fountain of Magic,* and *The Midnight Court.* With the first two books I had the help of W. B. Yeats. Indeed, wild horses could not have kept Yeats from helping with them, and sometimes, having supplied some felicitous line of his own, he promptly stole it back for one of his original poems. Hence the "influence" of these poems on Yeats's later work which Professor William York Tindall has pointed out. In the final drafts I have paid little attention to Yeats's suggestions, except in "Kilcash," where they seem to me not only to have enriched the poem, but also to have made it closer in feeling to the original.

Irish poetry has fared less well in translation than Latin and Greek but incomparably better than Welsh. In spite of the excellence of much Welsh poetry, no translation from it has merged into the common stock of English verse. Even in the early nineteenth century, Callanan, Ferguson, and Petrie each contributed one translation that is good poetry. Mangan's versions of Irish poems, like Rolleston's poem on Clonmacnois and Stephen's versions of O'Bruadair and

O'Rahilly can scarcely be called translations. They are fine original poems for which the material has been taken from Irish. Douglas Hyde's "My Grief on the Sea" is the perfect translation of a great poem from one language into another, and his "Ringleted Youth of My Love" runs it close. One or two of Colum's translations are in the same class. A few by Thomas McDonagh are excellent—particularly the early poem on "Eve"—though in the others there is a tendency toward schoolmaster elegance which becomes even more marked in the work of Robin Flower. In all great poetry, particularly in folk poetry, there is an element of ingenuousness, even of clumsiness, which the academic translator in his laudable desire to attach his poem to the corpus of accepted poetry tends to gloss over, forgetting that it is the acceptance of this very awkwardness which so often establishes a poem in the general mind. Perhaps Flower, being the only true scholar among our translators, knew his originals too well. There is only one disqualification worse than that, which is not knowing them well enough. Against the first disqualification I am well protected. I hope I have not neglected the second.

It is not an easy thing even for a scholar to fill in the background of these poems. Ireland was converted to Christianity from Britain probably during the fourth century and adopted the British type of church based on little hermit monasteries. In the following century St. Patrick completed the task in the northern part of Ireland, but his type of church, Roman and diocesan, never impinged on the basic British pattern. It is an important fact to remember when reading early Irish religious poetry.

The fall of the Roman Empire must have made Ireland for a time the last redoubt not only of the Celts but also of many citizens of the Empire. The remote hermitages of the early British and Irish saints—"little places taken first by twos and threes"—became folk colleges with substantial numbers of Anglo-Saxon and Frankish students. The pattern of life in these monasteries is clear from the architectural remains. Usually the monastery is in some wild and beautiful place, surrounded by a high wall of sods, and with half a dozen tiny oratories that were once linked up by streets of wooden houses. With the Danish invasions a watchtower is added with a doorway twelve or fifteen feet up, to which one could ascend only by a ladder. With the Hildebrandine Reformation, a larger church is added for no particular purpose except to call it a "cathedral." The monasteries were so many that it led to an emigration of monks. We need not exaggerate the intellectual quality of these monasteries—Professor Toynbee's picture of Ireland challenging Rome for the hegemony of Christianity is as farfetched as anything these fanciful Irishmen invented—but it was not mediocre, and it has left its mark on the religion of the Western world. The quality comes through in a handful of religious poems which, though they may have been written long after the events they describe, continue a tradition. (In fact the trouble with Ireland is that a tradition, once established, never stops.) The men of these poems, depending for all intellectual nourishment on their gospels and psalters, are those whom Bede described in England with admiration of their sanctity and bewilderment at their intellectual limitations. They were Dissenters, and had more than their share of Dissenting complacency. Their pattern was Christ, and the name rings out again and again in the poetry:

> *Christ, Christ hear me!*
> *Christ, Christ of Thy meekness!*
> *Christ, Christ, love me,*
> *Sever me not from Thy sweetness.*

Yet when we try to find out what sort of men these were in ordinary life, it is not to the Irish lives of them that we turn, for they are merely blasphemous buffoonery, but to Bede, who saw them at work, living exemplars of the imitation of Christ.

This introverted religion, with its inability to intellectualize itself, is paralleled in the literature by the sagas. These take a certain amount from Latin, and then proceed to handle it in a new and fascinating way. But because the literature has no such critical apparatus as Latin had, it fails to renew itself, and as texts are recopied every copyist's error, every word that in the meantime had lost its meaning, becomes a new stumbling block. Rationalisation—the curse of mediaeval literature—in Ireland becomes a monstrosity. A good example is the supposed "childbirth sickness" of the Ulstermen during which Cu Chulainn in the greatest of the Irish sagas defends the province, and this "childbirth sickness" created secondary sagas to explain it, and even today we find it in the work of modern scholars who try to account for it as a Celtic form of *couvade*. But the supposed *couvade* is merely an attempt at rationalising the Irish word *noinden*, which means *nundinae* or "festival" into *noiden*, which means 'baby.'

To a lesser degree, the same sort of thing takes place in the poetry. There were three main types of poetry in early Irish: court poetry, like "Carroll's Sword" and the epigrams on the death of various kings, written by professional poets; religious poetry, deriving more or less from Latin mediaeval poetry like "The Scholar and the Cat," and the incidental poetry of the sagas and romances like "Liadain." The poets took over Latin metrics and then proceeded to develop them in detail till they lost all sense of the architectonics of poetry and forgot that a poem, like any other work of art, must have a beginning, a middle, and an end. The unit of poetry became a quatrain, and this was polished until it turned into epigram. Although the epigrams that have come down to us are so very few, we can see that at one time Irish, like Welsh, was a poetry of epigram, and of some of those epigrams which have come down to us we can say, as Arnold said of the quatrains on Aengus the Culdee, that "a Greek epitaph could not show a finer perception of what constitutes propriety and felicity of style in compositions of this nature."

But though some of the religious poetry, like "A Prayer for Recollection" and "The Priest Rediscovers his Psalmbook," was written by men who knew that a poem had to have a beginning and an ending, "The Old Woman of Beare"—far finer poetry—was not; and it so obviously consists of quatrains that quatrains which have nothing to do with it were embodied in the text. What Rossetti called the "fundamental brainwork" is largely missing. Osborn Bergin, the great Celtic scholar, whose favourite Irish poem was the "Prayer for Recollection," maintained that it had the quality of intellect missing everywhere else in Irish. I think he felt that if only the Irish had studied this they would have learned how to beat the English. Their omission to do this was something a great scholar found it hard to forgive his ancestors for.

Another characteristic is the backward look. As I have hinted in the text, Irish poetry is haunted by the revenant, the figure who has escaped death only to return and find that Ireland, under the Christians, has gone to Hell. But this note characterises not only the Pagans, but also the Christians themselves. The hermit-poems, too, show the archaeologizing tendency because, like the poems dealing with the Fenians, they look back to a golden age. The Irish are like Orpheus, forever looking back at the Eurydice they are attempting to bring home from the Shades.

At the same time early Irish literature, whatever its faults, is, as Arnold would have said, "of the centre." It glows by its own light, the literature of a people full of confidence in itself. But the Danish invasions beginning in the ninth century soon shattered that confidence, and the chaos they produced got into the prose, as anyone can see from what was happening to the great national saga, "The Cattle Raid of Cuailgne," during the tenth and eleventh centuries. The old tense Latinized prose had become inflated with an appalling rhetoric that some scholars—God forgive them!—believe to have been always characteristic of the sagas.

There was a revival of culture which coincided with the Reformation of the twelfth century, an attempt to bring the Irish church into line with the European church which was itself a saga of considerable quality. But with the Norman invasion literature settled down to complete provincialism. This can be explained by the political situation, and the Norman pattern of life as architecture shows it to us. There is a square Norman castle beside a bridge, and a transitional church staffed by one of the foreign preaching orders, Dominican or Franciscan, who probably spoke with a Cockney version of French and tried to lord it over the Irish priests in a church five miles away, also beside a bridge and also protected by a castle of sorts. In both there would have been a court poet who wrote poems on his lord, Norman or Gaelic, though these would no longer have the old delight in style and would bear an even stronger resemblance to the poem written by the Mistress of Studies on Reverend Mother's feast day.

The intellectual decline is illustrated by churches that begin in some splendour, Transitional or Romanesque, and end in a composite form of architecture that represents the political triumph of the Irish chiefs and corresponds to the emergence of a Norman-Irish lyric poetry resembling, but not comparable with, the great outburst of Norman-Welsh poetry of Chaucer's day. The Irish had no Dafydd ap Gwilym.

But this poetry, like the architecture to which it corresponds, has real virtues. It is clean, spare, and functional—*démeublé* I believe is the word. It has nothing of the magic of early Irish poetry, either in its feeling for Nature or in its personal approach to religion. It is poetry in armour—the practical Irish armour of the period—and it has the intensity of everyday life, as though the men who had written it had done so while waiting for their horses to be saddled so that they might ride to some frontier post that a neighbour was attacking. It is the work of men who have lived intensely, but who have not travelled and have not read at all. After the Treaty of Limerick in 1691 and the departure of most of the Irish aristocracy to take service in France, Spain, and Austria, even this sort of poetry disappears, and its place is taken by folk poetry of various kinds.

"In Connacht," as I wrote in an earlier book, "there was genuine folk poetry, but in Munster the old world died in its sleep. The poetry of Egan O'Rahilly, David O'Bruadair and a hundred other peasant poets is that of the sleep-walker; their thought is so much of the old dead world that it is as though a veil had fallen between them and reality. When they speak English they are slaves: whining, cadging labouring men, but behind the barrier of their own language they move with their heads in clouds of romanticism."

Connacht folk poetry—though it belongs to the whole Gaelic world from the Highlands of Scotland to Cork—is a very different affair, rooted in the lives of the common people and dealing with simple and eternal things like girls without dowries, girls with illegitimate children, fathers who have lost their sons, and beggarmen, though all of them use the imagery and language of a great aristocratic tradition, and even a beggarman will end his song with some astonishing verse like

Would God that I and my darling
Were a thousand long leagues to the west,
In some island smothered with branches
Where all birds turn to their rest;
A place where the phoenix has nested,
Where eagle and cuckoo live gay—

'Tis there I'd put spells upon Phoebus
To take sunlight forever away.

Statistical evidence—in so far as I understand statistics—
shows that Anthony Raftery is the greatest poet in the
world, greater than Goethe and far greater than Shakespeare.
I have never been called on a quotation from Shakespeare;
twice I have been called on quotations from Goethe. Three
times I have been called on Raftery, the latest on the very
evening when I put finis to this book. I asked a waitress in a
Brooklyn restaurant where she came from and she replied:
"Mayo." I retorted with the first two lines of Raftery's
"County Mayo," and in perfect Irish she quoted:

I put my mind to it and I never will linger
Till I find myself back in the County Mayo.

That is proof positive, yet, God forgive me, I am bored
by Raftery. Merryman, the last of the great poets, is in a
different world entirely. Writing about 1790, he was deeply
influenced by the ideas of the Enlightenment and particu-
larly by Burns. (On his own statements the scholars believe
he came before Burns, but the thing is impossible. He must
derive from Burns.) Merryman at least was not afraid of the
fundamental brain-work of poetry. He had ideas about what
was wrong with Irish poetry and Irish life, and even if one
does not share them, one should admire the fierce intellec-
tual energy with which they are expressed. The translation
of his long poem is doubly banned in Ireland, and I believe
the best authorities hold that it is almost entirely my own
work, the one compliment Ireland ever has paid me. Had
Merryman been able to write in English—an English with
the magnificence of his Irish—his work would probably have
been more famous than that of Burns, for I think he was a

greater master of language; but the only aristocracy that could have given him an ear—the Anglo-Irish squireens of Maria Edgeworth's stories—like the aristocracy of Mr. De Valera, either could not or would not speak Irish, and, lacking an audience, he fell silent, a teacher of mathematics in a provincial town where no one knew him or cared for him. When he died in 1805 in a house on Clare Street, Limerick, Irish literature in the Irish language may be said to have died with him. From its beginnings among the monks of Clonmacnois and Glendalough to its end in Clare Street it was a literature of which no Irishman need feel ashamed.

Contents

Lords and Scholars   A.D. 1200–A.D. 1700

Peasants and Dreamers   A.D. 1600–A.D. 1800

Saints
and
Soldiers

A.D. 600–A.D. 1200

The Downfall of Heathendom

This is part of the great introduction to the Festology of Aengus the Spouse of God. The Spouses of God were an early Irish religious order, and the author expresses with amazing passion the self-confidence of the early Irish Church.

Ailill the king is vanished,
 Vanished Croghan's fort,
Kings to Clonmacnois
 Come to pay their court.

In quiet Clonmacnois
 About Saint Kieran's feet
Everlasting quires
 Raise a concert sweet.

Allen and its lords
 Both are overthrown,
Brigid's house is full,
 Far her fame has flown.

Navan town is shattered,
 Ruins everywhere;
Glendalough remains,
 Half a world is there.

Ferns is a blazing torch,
 Ferns is great and good,
But Beg, son of Owen,
 And his proud hosts are dead.

3

Old haunts of the heathen
    Filled from ancient days
Are but deserts now
    Where no pilgrim prays.

Little places taken
    First by twos and threes
Are like Rome reborn,
    Peopled sanctuaries.

Heathendom has gone down
    Though it was everywhere;
God the Father's kingdom
    Fills heaven and earth and air.

Sing the kings defeated!
    Sing the Donals down!
Clonmacnois triumphant,
    Cronan with the crown.

All the hills of evil,
    Level now they lie;
All the quiet valleys
    Tossed up to the sky.

The Hermitage

*This fine poem is ascribed to St. Manchan of Lemana-
ghan in Offaly, which takes its name from him, but it
is some centuries after his time. It is an interesting ex-
ample of the backward-looking tendency of Irish litera-
ture, religious and secular.*

Grant me sweet Christ the grace to find—
    Son of the living God!—
A small hut in a lonesome spot
    To make it my abode.

A little pool but very clear
    To stand beside the place
Where all men's sins are washed away
    By sanctifying grace.

A pleasant woodland all about
    To shield it from the wind,
And make a home for singing birds
    Before it and behind.

A southern aspect for the heat,
    A stream along its foot,
A smooth green lawn with rich top soil
    Propitious to all fruit.

My choice of men to live with me
    And pray to God as well;
Quiet men of humble mind—
    Their number I shall tell.

Four files of three or three of four
    To give the psalter forth;
Six to pray by the south church wall
    And six along the north.

Two by two my dozen friends—
    To tell the number right—
Praying with me to move the King
    Who gives the sun its light.

A lovely church, a home for God,
    Bedecked with linen fine,
Where over the white Gospel page
    The Gospel candles shine.

A little house where all may dwell
    And body's care be sought,
Where none shows lust or arrogance,
    None thinks an evil thought.

And all I ask for housekeeping
    I get and pay no fees,
Leeks from the garden, poultry, game,
    Salmon and trout and bees.

My share of clothing and of food
    From the King of fairest face,
And I to sit at times alone
    And pray in every place.

The Hermit's Song

These verses are from a poetic discussion on the religious life between King Guaire and his hermit brother, Marbhan, both of the seventh century. Here, too, the poet is looking back. It is extraordinary how clear and bright the landscape of early Irish poetry is, as though some mediaeval painter had illustrated it, with its little oratories hung with linen, its woodlands and birds, its fierce winters and gay springs.

A hiding tuft, a green-barked yew-tree
    Is my roof,
While nearby a great oak keeps me
    Tempest-proof.

I can pick my fruit from an apple
    Like an inn,
Or can fill my fist where hazels
    Shut me in.

A clear well beside me offers
    Best of drink,
And there grows a bed of cresses
    Near its brink.

Pigs and goats, the friendliest neighbours,
    Nestle near,
Wild swine come, or broods of badgers,
    Grazing deer.

All the gentry of the county
    Come to call!
And the foxes come behind them,
    Best of all.

To what meals the woods invite me
    All about!
There are water, herbs and cresses,
    Salmon, trout.

A clutch of eggs, sweet mast and honey
    Are my meat,
Heathberries and whortleberries
    For a sweet.

All that one could ask for comfort
    Round me grows,
There are hips and haws and strawberries,
    Nuts and sloes.

And when summer spreads its mantle
    What a sight!
Marjoram and leeks and pignuts,
    Juicy, bright.

Dainty redbreasts briskly forage
    Every bush,
Round and round my hut there flutter
    Swallow, thrush.

Bees and beetles, music-makers,
    Croon and strum;
Geese pass over, duck in autumn,
    Dark streams hum.

Angry wren, officious linnet
    And black-cap,
All industrious, and the woodpeckers'
    Sturdy tap.

From the sea the gulls and herons
    Flutter in,
While in upland heather rises
    The grey hen.

In the year's most brilliant weather
    Heifers low
Through green fields, not driven nor beaten,
    Tranquil slow.

In wreathed boughs the wind is whispering,
    Skies are blue,
Swans call, river water falling
    Is calling too.

A Prayer for Recollection

How my thoughts betray me!
How they flit and stray!
Well they may appal me
On great judgment day.

Through the psalms they wander
Roads that are not right;
Mitching, shouting, squabbling
In God's very sight.

Through august assemblies
Groups of gamesome girls,
Then through woods, through cities,
Like the wind in whirls.

Now down lordly highways
Boisterously they stride,
Then through desert pathways
Secretly they glide.

In their whims unferried
Overseas they fly,
Or in one swift motion
Spin from earth to sky.

Lost to recollection
Near and far they roam;
From some monstrous errand
Slyly they slink home.

Where are ropes to bind them?
Who has fetters fit?
They who lack all patience
Cannot stand or sit.

No sharp sword affrights them,
      Nor any threatening whip;
Like an eel's tail, greasy,
      From my grasp they slip.

Lock nor frowning dungeon,
      Nor sentinelled frontier,
Townwall, sea nor fortress
      Halts their mad career.

Christ the chaste, the cherished,
      Searcher of the soul,
Grant the seven-fold spirit
      Keep them in control.

Rule my thoughts and feelings,
      You who brook no ill;
Make me yours forever,
      Bend me to your will.

Grant me, Christ, to reach you,
      With you let me be
Who are not frail nor fickle
      Nor feeble-willed like me.

The Priest Rediscovers His Psalm-Book

This exquisite poem gave rise to a two-volume work by George Moore called A Storyteller's Holiday, *which celebrates the* virgines subintroductae *of the early Irish church. The* virgines subintroductae *were the women who accompanied early saints, but if there were any in Ireland, Crinog, the heroine of this poem was not one of them. Her name, which means "Old-Young," is merely a typical donnish joke as a modern scholar, Mr. Carney, has shown.*

How good to hear your voice again,
    Old love, no longer young, but true,
As when in Ulster I grew up
    And we were bedmates, I and you.

When first they put us twain to bed,
    My love who speaks the tongue of Heaven,
I was a boy with no bad thoughts,
    A modest youth, and barely seven.

We wandered Ireland over then,
    Our souls and bodies free of blame,
My foolish face aglow with love,
    An idiot without fear of blame.

Yours was the counsel that I sought
    Wherever we went wandering;
Better I found your subtle thought
    Than idle converse with some king.

You slept with four men after that,
    Yet never sinned in leaving me,
And now a virgin you return—
    I say but what all men can see.

For safe within my arms again,
　　Weary of wandering many ways,
The face I love is shadowed now
　　Though lust attends not its last days.

Faultless my old love seeks me out;
　　I welcome her with joyous heart—
My dear, you would not have me lost,
　　With you I'll learn that holy art.

Since all the world your praises sings,
　　And all acclaim your wanderings past
I have but to heed your counsel sweet
　　To find myself with God at last.

You are a token and a sign
　　To men of what all men must heed;
Each day your lovers learn anew
　　God's praise is all the skill they need.

So may He grant me by your grace
　　A quiet end, an easy mind,
And light my pathway with His face
　　When the dead flesh is left behind.

The Scholar and the Cat

This, one of the most beautiful poems of the early Middle Ages, was found in a manuscript in Austria. I have hinted at the rhyme-scheme of the Irish, which displaces the accent in alternate lines. Robin Flower's well-known translation in the metre of "Twinkle, twinkle, little star" ignores the slowness of the original, which approximates more to iambic pentameter.

Each of us pursues his trade,
I and Pangur my comrade,
His whole fancy on the hunt,
And mine for learning ardent.

More than fame I love to be
Among my books and study,
Pangur does not grudge me it,
Content with his own merit.

When—a heavenly time!—we are
In our small room together
Each of us has his own sport
And asks no greater comfort.

While he sets his round sharp eye
On the wall of my study
I turn mine, though lost its edge,
On the great wall of knowledge.

Now a mouse drops in his net
After some mighty onset
While into my bag I cram
Some difficult darksome problem.

When a mouse comes to the kill
Pangur exults, a marvel!
I have when some secret's won
My hour of exultation.

Though we work for days and years
Neither the other hinders;
Each is competent and hence
Enjoys his skill in silence.

Master of the death of mice,
He keeps in daily practice,
I too, making dark things clear,
Am of my trade a master.

1 The Open Door

> King of stars,
> > Dark or bright my house may be,
> But I close my door on none
> > Lest Christ close his door on me.

2 A Word of Warning

> To go to Rome
> > Is little profit, endless pain;
> The Master that you seek in Rome,
> > You find at home, or seek in vain.

3 Scholars

> Strange is it not if scholars yell
> In torment on the hob of hell
> While louts who never learned their letters
> Are perched in Heaven above their betters?

The Sweetness of Nature

*This is one of the songs of the mad king, Suibhne
(Sweeney) from a twelfth-century romance, the material
of which goes back to the eighth century. In this poem
Suibhne is flying from the battlefield, driven mad by the
sight of the broken bodies. To me the whole romance
seems to have some obscure connection with the Hamlet
legend.*

Endlessly over the water
    Birds of the Bann are singing;
Sweeter to me their voices
    Than any churchbell's ringing.

Over the plain of Moyra
    Under the heels of foemen
I saw my people broken
    As flax is scutched by women.

But the cries I hear by Derry
    Are not of men triumphant;
I hear their calls in the evening,
    Swans calm and exultant.

I hear the stag's belling
    Over the valley's steepness;
No music on the earth
    Can move me like its sweetness.

Christ, Christ hear me!
    Christ, Christ of Thy meekness!
Christ, Christ love me!
    Sever me not from Thy sweetness!

May's the merriest time of all,
    Life comes back to everything,
While a ray of light remains
    The never weary blackbirds sing.

That's the cuckoo's strident voice,
    "Welcome summer great and good!"
All the fury of the storm
    Lost in tangles of the wood.

Summer stems the languid stream,
    Thirsty horses rush the pool,
Bracken bristles everywhere,
    White bog-cotton is in bloom.

Scant of breath the burdened bees
    Carry home the flowery spoil,
To the mountains go the cows,
    The ant is glutted with his meal.

The wind awakes the woodland's harp,
    The sail falls and the world's at rest,
A mist of heat upon the hills
    And the water full of mist.

The corncake drones, a bustling bard,
    The cold cascade that leaps the rock
Sings of the snugness of the pool,
    Their season come, the rushes talk.

The man grows strong, the virgin tall,
    Each in his glory, firm and light,
Bright the far and fertile plain,
    Bright the wood from floor to height.

Here among the meadowlands
  An eager flock of birds descends,
And there a stream runs white and fast
  Where the murmuring meadow bends.

And you long to race a horse
  Headlong through the parting crowd,
The sun has scarcely touched the land
  But the water-flags are gold.

Frightened, foolish, frail, a bird
  Sings of it with throbbing breast—
The lark that flings its praise abroad,
  May the brightest and the best.

Chill, chill!
All Moylurg is cold and still,
Where can deer a-hungered go
When the snow lies like a hill?

Cold till doom!
All the world obeys its rule,
Every track become a stream,
Every ford become a pool.

Every pool become a lake,
Every lake become a sea,
Even horses cannot cross
The ford at Ross so how can we?

All the fish in Ireland stray
When the cold winds smite the bay,
In the towns no voice is heard,
Bell and bird have had their say.

Even the wolves in Cuan Wood
Cannot find a place to rest
When the small wren of Lon Hill
Is not still within her nest.

The small quire of birds has passed
In cold snow and icy blast,
And the blackbird of Cuan Wood
Finds no shelter that holds fast.

Nothing's easy but our pot,
Our old shack on the hill is not,
For in woodlands crushed with snow
On Ben Bo the trail's forgot.

The old eagle of Glen Rye,
Even he forgets to fly,
With ice crusted on his beak,
He is now too weak to cry.

Best lie still
In wool and feathers, take your fill,
Ice is thick on every ford
And the word I chose is "chill."

Storm at Sea

The ascription of this comparatively late poem to an eighth-century poet, Rumann son of Colman, suggests that it may be part of a romance that dealt with him.

Tempest on the plain of Lir
Bursts its barriers far and near,
   And upon the rising tide
   Wind and noisy winter ride—
Winter throws a shining spear.

When the wind blows from the east
All the billows seem possessed,
   To the west they storm away
   To the farthest, wildest bay
Where the light turns to its rest.

When the wind is from the north
The fierce and shadowy waves go forth,
   Leaping, snarling at the sky,
   To the southern world they fly
And the confines of the earth.

When the wind is from the west
All the waves that cannot rest
   To the east must thunder on
   Where the bright tree of the sun
Is rooted in the ocean's breast.

When the wind is from the south
The waves turn to a devil's broth,
   Crash in foam on Skiddy's beach,
   For Caladnet's summit reach,
Batter Limerick's grey-green mouth.

Ocean's full! The sea's in flood,
Beautiful is the ships' abode;
    In the Bay of the Two Beasts
    The sandy wind in eddies twists,
The rudder holds a shifting road.

Every bay in Ireland booms
When the flood against it comes—
    Winter throws a spear of fire!
    Round Scotland's shores and by Cantyre
A mountainous surging chaos glooms.

God's Son of hosts that none can tell
The fury of the storm repel!
    Dread Lord of the sacrament,
    Save me from the wind's intent,
Spare me from the blast of Hell.

Look, wild and wide,
Northeast, the tide
Beneath which bide
        The dragons' brood,
The seals' delight,
All foam and light,
Mounts to full height—
        The sea's in flood!

Autumn

This, like the similar poem on Winter, is a story-poem that tells how an Irish poet was detained on a visit through the four seasons by his foster-son's praise of them.

Autumn's good, a cosy season;
Then there's work for man and woman,
While each day the sunlight dwindles
Speckled fawn through reddening bracken
    Scatter from the herd.

Stags leap up from sandy hollows
Answering the hind's deep bellow,
Acorns drop in peaceful woodlands,
Corn stands up in golden plenty
    Over the brown world.

Even the spiky thorn-bush growing
By the old deserted fortress
Staggers with its weight of berries,
Hazel nuts thud in the forest
    From the wearied boughs.

Winter is a dreary season,
Heavy waters in confusion
    Beat the wide world's strand.
Birds of every place are mournful
But the hot and savage ravens,
    At rough winter's shriek.
Crude and black and dank and smoky;
Dogs about their bones are snarling,
On the fire the cauldron bubbles
    All the long dark day.

The Blackbird by Belfast Lough

What little throat
Has framed that note?
What gold beak shot
    It far away?
A blackbird on
His leafy throne
Tossed it alone
    Across the bay.

The Praise of Fionn

*Usheen ("Oisin" or "Ossian"), son of Fionn, is the great
revenant of Irish literature. Translated to the Land of
Youth by his love of a fairy queen, he returned to Ire-
land to find Fionn and his warriors long dead and St.
Patrick and his monks in power. Although the poem is
late so far as language goes—probably sixteenth-century
—it has the feeling of the eighth or ninth century.*

Patrick you chatter too loud
    And lift your crozier too high,
Your stick would be kindling soon
    If my son Osgar stood by.

If my son Osgar and God
    Wrestled it out on the hill
And I saw Osgar go down
    I'd say that your God fought well.

But how could the God you praise
    And his mild priests singing a tune
Be better then Fionn the swordsman,
    Generous, faultless Fionn?

Just by the strength of their hands
    The Fenians' battles were fought,
With never a spoken lie,
    Never a lie in thought.

There never sat priest in church
    A tuneful psalm to raise
Better spoken than these
    Scarred in a thousand frays.

Whatever your monks have called
    The law of the King of Grace,
That was the Fenians' law;
    His home is their dwelling-place.

If happier house than Heaven
    There be, above or below,
'Tis there my master Fionn
    And his fighting men will go.

Ah, priest, if you saw the Fenians
    Filling the strand beneath
Or gathered in streamy Naas
    You would praise them with every breath.

Patrick, ask of your God
    Does he remember their might,
Or has he seen east or west
    Better men in a fight?

Or known in his own land
    Above the stars and the moon
For wisdom, courage and strength
    A man the like of Fionn?

The teeth you see up here,
    Up in the ancient skull,
Once cracked yellow nuts
    And tore the haunch of a bull.

Savage and sharp and huge,
    Crunching the naked bone,
Every tittle and joint
    Was mince when they were done.

The eyes you see up here,
    Up in the aged skull,
Dull they may seem tonight
    But once they were never dull.

Never in darkest night
    Did they take trip or fall;
Now, though you stand so close,
    I cannot see you at all.

The legs you see below,
    Nothing could weary them then;
Now they totter and ache,
    A bundle of bones and skin.

Though now they run no more,
    All their glory gone,
Once they were quick to follow
    The shadow of golden Fionn.

Caoilte

Caoilte is another of the revenant figures who return to an Ireland where, because of St. Patrick, everything seems to have become cheapened and diminished. "Osgar," who is celebrated in "The Praise of Fionn," is the son of Oisin and grandson of Fionn, and "Diarmuid," the Tristan of Irish legend, is the hero of another poem, "Grania."

Winter time is bleak, the wind
    Drives the stag from height to height;
Belling at the mountain's cold
    Untameable he strays tonight.

The old stag of Carran scarce
    Dare sleep within his den,
While the stag of Aughty hears
    Wolves call in every glen.

Long ago Osgar and I
    And Diarmuid heard that cry;
And we listened to the wolves
    As the frosty night went by.

Now the stag that's filled with sleep
    Lays his lordly side to rest
As if earth had drawn him down
    To the winter's icy breast.

Though I drowse above the fire
    Many a winter morning drear
My hand was tight about a sword
    A battleaxe or spear.

And though I sleep cold tonight,
    God, I offer thanks to you
And to Christ, the Virgin's Son,
    For the mighty men I slew.

Generosity

Fionn, the Celtic god from whom Vienna and Vienne both take their names, is humanized (euhemerized is the technical term) in Ireland into a leader of a warrior band, the Fianna or Fenians. A great deal of Irish literature is devoted to contrasting the ideal heroes of the pagan world with the clerics by whom they were followed.

If only the brown leaf were gold
The wood sheds when the year is old,
Or if the waves had silver spray
These too would Fionn have given away.

The Old Woman of Beare

The Old Woman of Beare (in County Cork) is one of the standard revenant figures of early Irish literature, a goddess who, having survived for long ages, finds herself a nun in a Christian community. "Femuin" and "Bregon" are both in the vicinity of Cashel, County Tipperary.

I, the old woman of Beare
Once a shining shift would wear,
Now and since my beauty's fall
I have scarce a shift at all.

Plump no more I sigh for these
Bones bare beyond belief;
Ebbtide is all my grief,
I am ebbing like the seas.

It is pay
And not men ye love today,
But when we were young, ah, then
We gave all our hearts to men.

Men most dear,
Horseman, huntsman, charioteer;
We gave them love with all our will
But the measure did not fill.

Though today they ask so fine,
And small good they get of it;
They are worn-out in their prime
By the little that they get.

And long since the foaming steed
And the chariot with its speed
And the charioteer went by—
God be with them all say I.

Luck has left me, I go late
To the dark house where they wait;
When the Son of God thinks fit
Let Him call me home to it.

For my hands as you may see
Are but bony wasted things,
Hands that once would grasp the hand
Clasp the royal neck of kings.

Oh, my hands as may be seen
Are so scraggy and so thin
That a boy might start in dread
Feeling them about his head.

Girls are gay
When the year draws on to May,
But for me, so poor am I,
Sun will scarcely light the day.

Not mine now sweet words to say,
Not for me the wether dies,
While my hair is short and grey
This poor veil is no surprise.

Though I care
Nothing for what binds my hair,
I had headgear bright enough
When the kings for love went bare.

'Tis not age that makes my pain
But the eye that sees so plain
How when all it loves decays
Femuin's ways are gold again.

Femuin, Bregon, sacring stone,
Sacring stone and Ronan's throne
Storms have sacked so long that now
Tomb and sacring stone are one.

Winter overwhelms the land,
The waves are noisy on the strand,
So I may not hope today
Prince or slave will come my way.

Where are they? Ah, well I know
Old and toiling bones that row
Almas's flood, or by its deep
Sleep in cold that slept not so.

Welladay!
That I am no girl today;
All my beauty to my cost,
Lost, with all my will to play.

And O God!
Once again for ill or good
Spring will come, and I shall see
Everything but me renewed.

Summer sun and autumn sun,
These I knew, and they are gone,
And the winter-time of men
Comes, and they come not again.

Madly did I spend my prime,
What is there to cause me rage?
If in prayer I had passed the time,
Should I be less grieved at age?

And "Amen!" I cry and "Woe
"That the boughs are shaken bare!
"And that candlelight and feast
"Leave me to the dark and prayer!"

I who had my day with kings
And drank deep of mead and wine
Drink wheywater with old hags
Sitting in their rags and pine.

"That my cups be cups of whey!
"That Thy will be done!" I pray,
But the prayer, O Living God,
Wakes a madness in my blood.

And I cry "Your locks are grey"
To the mantle that I stroke;
Then I grieve and murmur, "Nay,
"I am grey and not my cloak."

And of eyes that loved the sun
Age, my grief, has taken one,
And the other too will take
Soon for good proportion's sake.

Floodtide!
Flood or ebb upon the strand!
What the floodtide brings to you
Ebbtide carries from my hand.

Floodtide!
Ebbtide with the hurrying fall!
All have reached me, ebb and flow,
Ay, and now I know them all.

Floodtide!
Cannot reach me where I call;
None in darkness seeks my side,
Cold the hand that lies on all.

Happy island of the main
To you the tide will come again,
But to me it comes no more
Over the blank, deserted shore.

Seeing it, I can scarcely say
"This was such a place," today
What was water far and wide
Changes with the ebbing tide.

The Song of the Heads

This, one of many fine story-poems, illustrates the development of the ballad. The speaker is supposed to be one of three poet brothers who had planned to celebrate the victory of Cormac, King of Cashel.

Alas, O King of Kings,
Righteous lord of might
The saddest of songs we sing,
Heads in the bitter night.

Come hither, Gegan's head,
Together let us sing.
Have you and I not said
We would make a song for the king?

Last evening our hearts were light,
We stood in a goodly throng,
We are but three heads tonight,
Singing a lonely song.

Last night at supper the King
Pledged us, one by one,
A song of triumph to sing
Tonight with the battle won.

Alas for the sport and the crowds,
Though short a night and a day
In less, the King of the clouds
Can turn the mighty to clay.

Alas for glory and mirth,
Cormac himself was struck down,
His seed has perished from earth,
Lost is Cashel's renown.

Cormac from the hill of state
      Ruled Munster crop and herd,
The poor man and the great
      Obeyed his lightest word.

Vats were raised in a row,
      Woodlands of oak-trees bowed,
Princes were laid low
      And beggars were made proud.

Now, have done with your song,
      A last farewell. It is day,
Back to where we belong
      With the cold stones and the clay.

Carroll's Sword

Court poetry is a peculiar and unattractive form, and to me always reminiscent of an illuminated address or a song for Reverend Mother's feast day. But every great Irish family kept a poem-book in the way in which we keep photograph albums. Early court poetry—particularly the poetry in epigram—is relatively fresh. Carroll was King of Leinster at the end of the ninth century.

O swinging sword of Carroll hail!
Often the shuttle of the war,
  Often sustaining fight,
  Splitting the necks of kings.

Often abroad on plunder bent,
Companion of sagacious lords,
  Often sharing a spoil
  With kings who shared your worth.

Often sustained by some bright hand
Where Leinstermen were gathered in,
  Often in mighty hosts,
  Often with princely stock.

Many the masters that you served,
For whom you plied a stirring fight;
  Many the shield you clove,
  The breast, the skull, the skin.

For forty years unstained with grief
With Enda of the surging hosts—
  You never faced a fight
  But in some fierce king's hand.

To Dowling Enda gave you up,
To his own son—no trifling gift;
    Him you served thirty years
    And brought him death at last.

Many a king on mettled horse
Before you stepped at Diarmuid's side,
    And so for sixteen years
    You were his prop in war.

At Allen's fair you changed your lords;
Grim Diarmuid yielded you in turn;
    The good king passed you on
    To Murigan of Marg.

Another forty years you passed
In the strong hand of Allen's king,
    No year without a fight
    For mighty Murigan.

In Wexford from the Danish king's
You passed to Carroll's hand at last:
    Carroll gave you to none
    While the gold earth he trod.

Crimson he dyed your bright blue point
In Ogva of the Foreigners;
    You left Hugh Findlay low
    In Ogva of wide paths.

That edge of yours was blooded too
In Balagh Moon, your worth approved,
    And in Moy Alvey's fight
    When desperate deeds were done.

On Thursday at Dun Oughter's charge
Before you broke the splendid host,
    When brave and boisterous Hugh
    Was left dead on the hill.

The day that Kelly fell, from you
The great battalion rushed in flight;
    The son of Flanagan
    At lofty Tara slain.

But day of rout you never knew
With Carroll of the gracious guards
    Who never swore untruth,
    Never his word belied.

No day of mourning did you know
But many a night of war-faring;
    You had good lords, good luck
    And many a brilliant fight.

But who can now the trust maintain
Or whom in ruin will you smite?
    Now Carroll lives no more
    Who'll share his bed with you?

You need not fear, you will not stray
Till Naas in triumph see you come
    Where Fionn of feasts is throned
    There they shall cry "All hail!"

Dallan Mac More

The King of Connacht

This, one of the great epitaphs of history, is quoted in Kuno Meyer's Primer of Irish Metrics *as an example of* Mimasc, 4/3 + 6/1.

"Have you seen Hugh,
The Connacht king in the field?"
"All that we saw
Was his shadow under his shield."

The Viking Terror

In London during the Second World War we waited for a moonlit night to sleep safe in our beds. In Ireland of the ninth century they waited for a storm.

Since tonight the wind is high,
The sea's white mane a fury
I need not fear the hordes of Hell
Coursing the Irish Channel.

The End of Clonmacnois

*In the Second World War, Oxford escaped destruction,
but Ireland of the ninth century was not so lucky. To
the people of the time, Clonmacnois meant what Oxford
means to an Englishman, Harvard to an American.
For Swords read, perhaps, Barrow-on-Furness or Seat-
tle. The main point is that this is not an epigram on a
minor historical event.*

"Whence are you, learning's son?"
"From Clonmacnois I come.
"My course of studies done,
        "I'm off to Swords again."
"How are things keeping there?"
"Oh, things are shaping fair—
"Foxes round churchyards bare
        "Gnawing the guts of men."

Murrough Defeats the Danes, 994

Ye people of great Murrough's band,
Unstayed by wood or moorland,
Panic seized the Danish hordes
Before your sunbright standards;
Their noses drip with snow in flight
O'er Aughty in the twilight.

The King of Ulster

Kuno Meyer identifies the Conor of this poem as king of Tirkeeran near Londonderry, circa 1096.

Conor the king
As little heeds
His wagon packed
        With Danish loot
As in the woods
In Autumn God
Heeds how He drops
        The golden fruit.

Grania

Grania is the original Iseult of the Tristan legend. Married to the elderly Fionn, she drugged the watchmen's drink and eloped with her lover Diarmuid. In the Lullaby we are to understand that they are being followed by Fionn and the Fianna, whose quest has set all nature in a tumult, but she sings Diarmuid to sleep with memories of the great lovers of Irish history.

This was the basis of Yeats's beautiful "Lullaby," which he wrote after reading my first version of the poem. But I was never satisfied with that; nor am I particularly satisfied with this, except that it is closer in spirit to the original.

Stag does not lay his side to sleep;
    He bellows from the mountainside,
And tramples through the woods, and yet
    In no green thicket can he hide.

Not even the birds within their house—
    From bough to bough all night they leap,
And stir the air with startled cries.
    Among the leaves they will not sleep.

The duck that bears her brood tonight
    By many a sheltering bank must creep,
And furrow the wild waters bright;
    Among the reeds she will not sleep.

The curlew cannot sleep at all
    His voice is shrill above the deep
Reverberations of the storm;
    Between the streams he will not sleep.

But you must sleep as in the south
        He who from Conall long ago
With all the arts of speech and song
        Made Morann's daughter rise and go.

Or sleep the sleep that Fionncha found
        In Ulster with his stolen bride,
When Slaney ran from home with him
        And slept no more at Falvey's side.

Or sleep the sleep that Aunya slept
        When with the torchlight round her head,
From Garnish and her father's house
        To her beloved's arms she fled.

Or Dedaid's sleep who in the east
        Did not think for one sweet night,
His head upon his lover's breast
        Of the terrors of the flight.

Liadain

Liadain ("the grey lady") was a Munster poetess who, according to the romance, was courted by another poet, Curithir ("Otter's Son") with the remarkable plea—"a child of ours should be famous." Because, as the romance makes clear, she did not wish to spoil her round of visits, she asked him to join her at home in Munster, but when he arrived, she had already become a nun. In the same romance she is given an equally wonderful but untranslatable poem in which she describes him as "the ex-poet." Only those who have known an ex-poet will realise what the word means.

Gain without gladness
    Is in the bargain I have struck;
One that I loved I wrought to madness.

Mad beyond measure
    But for God's fear that numbed her heart
She that would not do his pleasure.

Was it so great
    My treason? Was I not always kind?
Why should it turn his love to hate?

Liadain,
    That is my name, and Curithir
The man I loved; you know my sin.

Alas too fleet!
    Too brief my pleasure at his side;
With him the passionate hours were sweet.

Woods woke
    About us for a lullaby,
And the blue waves in music spoke.

And now too late
    More than for all my sins I grieve
That I turned his love to hate.

Why should I hide
    That he is still my heart's desire
More than all the world beside?

A furnace blast
    Of love has melted down my heart,
Without his love it cannot last.

Men and Women

1 Kiss

He's my doll!
 I'm so dim!
I send this
 Kiss for him.

2 The Goldsmith's Wife

The goldsmith's wife
 Is blacksmith-bred
With a face too white
 And a cheek too red.

3 Aideen

All are keen
To known who'll sleep with blond Aideen,
All Aideen herself will own
Is that she will not sleep alone.

4 No Names

There's a girl in these parts—
 A remarkable thing!
But the force of her farts
 Is like stones from a sling.

5 All Gold

Hero's daughter, Leinster's loveliest!
 Child of kings!
Mingling in one glow her ringlets
 And her rings.

What happier fortune can one find
Than with the girl who pleased one's mind
To leave one's home and friends behind
And sail on the first favouring wind?

Lords
and
Scholars

A.D. 1200–A.D. 1700

A Learned Mistress

It is part of the legend of Irish history that the Renais-
sance missed Ireland completely, but Ireland was a part,
however minute, of Europe, and in their dank and
smoky castles, the Irish and Anglo-Irish aristocracy lived
a life that fundamentally differed little from the life that
went on in the castles of the Loire. Isobel Campbell, the
great countess of Argyle, wrote a poem to her chaplain's
—but really, I can't say what—and the joke was taken
up by her Campbell kinsmen, who still wrote classical
Irish. She might have written this little poem, and who
will dare to say that it does not breathe the whole spirit
of the Renaissance?

> Tell him it's all a lie;
>> I love him as much as my life;
> He needn't be jealous of me—
>> I love him and loathe his wife.

> If he kill me through jealousy now
>> His wife will perish of spite,
> *He'*ll die of grief for his wife—
>> Three of us dead in a night.

> All blessings from heaven to earth
>> On the head of the woman I hate,
> And the man I love as my life,
>> Sudden death be his fate.

She Is My Dear

She is my dear
Who makes me weep so many a tear,
    And whom I love far more for it
Than one who only brings good cheer.

She is my own,
Day in day out she hears me groan,
    And does not care if I am sad
And would not grieve if I were gone.

She is my delight
She whose dear eyes are ever bright,
    Whose hand will never prop my head,
Who will not turn to me at night.

She is my all
Who tells me nothing, great or small,
    And does not see me when I pass
And does not hear me when I call.

I Shall Not Die

I shall not die because of you
    O woman though you shame the swan,
They were foolish men you killed,
    Do not think me a foolish man.

Why should I leave the world behind
    For the soft hand, the dreaming eye,
The crimson lips, the breasts of snow—
    Is it for these you'd have me die?

Why should I heed the fancy free,
    The joyous air, the eye of blue,
The side like foam, the virgin neck?
    I shall not die because of you.

The devil take the golden hair!
    That maiden look, that voice so gay,
That delicate heel and pillared thigh
    Only some foolish man would slay.

O woman though you shame the swan
    A wise man taught me all he knew,
I know the crooked ways of love,
    I shall not die because of you.

Growing Old

This little poem, improbably ascribed to various poets, is the perfection of the "functional" type of poetry. A poem could hardly be more démeublé *than this.*

Woman full of wile
Take your hand away,
Nothing tempts me now,
Sick for love you pray.

But my hair is grey
And my flesh is weak,
All my blood gone cold—
What is it you seek?

Do not think me mad,
Do not hang your head,
Slender witch let love
Live in thought not deed.

Take your mouth from mine,
Kissing's bitterer still,
Flesh from flesh must part
Lest of warmth come will.

Your twined branching hair,
Your grey eye dew-bright,
Your rich rounded breast
Turn to lust the sight.

But for the wild bed
And the body's flame,
Woman full of wile
My love is still the same.

Retirement

In youth I served my time
    To kissing and love-making;
Now that I must retire
    I feel my heart is breaking.

Love's a great trade indeed;
    I have loved and cannot doubt it.
That I should live is strange
    For life's a waste without it—

And memory makes a torment
    Of all my past blisses—
Ah, God, ah God! 'tis food today
    That feeds me and not kisses.

Love and Hate

Hate only will I love,
    Love I will set aside,
The misery of love
    Too many a heart has tried.

My scorn upon the thing
    That such vain grief began
And many a good man made
    Into a sick man.

Even when it goes too far
    Hate's the better part,
One can bid Hate pack,
    Who can bid love depart?

Hate is healthy fare
    That leaves the body sound,
Nor herb nor medicine cures
    Love's bitter wound.

Once I saw a girl
    Choose a man in play;
Love he never knew
    To his dying day.

I whate'er befall
    Know a better fate—
This is all my song,
    I will love only hate.

Death and the Maiden

My girl I say be on your guard
   And put folly from your head,
Take my counsel and be hard,
   Think of me and do not wed.

Though you scorn advice today
   When your cheeks are bright and red
And you do not know my way,
   Think of me and do not wed.

Me? Yourself you do not know,
   Never saw yourself in dread,
Pillared throat and breasts of snow—
   Think of me and do not wed.

Give no man your love or hate,
   Leave the foolish words unsaid,
Spare your kisses, they can wait—
   Think of me and do not wed.

Think of me and do not wed,
   Let the road be smooth or hard,
I shall be there when all are fled—
   My girl, I say be on your guard.

A Jealous Man

Listen jealous man
    What they say of you
That you watch your wife
    Surely isn't true?

Such an ugly face
    The light loves disown;
Much to your surprise
    Your wife is all your own.

Other men must watch
    Who have wives to shield,
Why should you put up
    A fence without a field?

In a hundred none
    Is as safe as you
Nobody could think
    Such a thing was true.

Men cry when they're hurt,
    Your cry's out of place,
Who do you think would want
    Such an ugly face?

A Man of Experience

Really, what a shocking scene!
    A decent girl, a public place!
What the devil do you mean,
    Mooching round with such a face!

Things can't really be so bad,
    Surely someone would have said
If—of course the thing is mad,
    No, your mother isn't dead.

Sighing, sniffling, looking tense,
    Sitting mum the whole day through;
Speaking from experience
    I can guess what's wrong with you.

Roses withering in the cheek,
    Sunlight clouding in the hair,
Heaving breasts and looks so meek—
    You're in love, my girl, I swear.

If love really caused all this
    So that looks and grace are gone
Shouldn't you tell me who it is?—
    Even if I should be the man.

If I really were the man
    You wouldn't find me too severe,
Don't think I'm a Puritan,
    I've been through it too my dear.

And if you'd whispered in my ear:
    "Darling, I'm in love with you"
I wouldn't have scolded, never fear;
    I know just what girls go through.

How does it take you, could you say?
    Are you faint when I pass by?
Don't just blush and look away—
    Who should know love if not I?

You'll be twice the girl tonight
    Once you get if off your chest;
Why—who knows?—you even might
    Win me to your snowy breast.

Make love just the way that seems
    Fittest to you, 'twill be right.
Think of it! Your wildest dreams
    Might come true this very night.

That's enough for once, my dear
    Stop that snivelling and begin;
Come now, not another tear—
    Lord, look at the state you're in!

Laoiseach Mac an Bhaird

The Vanished Night

God be with the night that's gone!
   Long the day it ushered in;
If ever I be crucified
   Tonight my torments should begin.

A pair within this house tonight
   Have secrets that their eyes express.
Long, ah long the looks they mingle
   As though they lingered in a kiss!

Silence is what tells the tale
   Of the love their lips conceal
Why should silence seek to veil
   Secrets that the eyes reveal?

O eyes I love, the mockers' tongues
   Have kept me silent in your sight,
But look in mine! They cry aloud
   The words I whispered in the night.

"Keep tomorrow night for me!
   "Could we but always live this way!
"Do not let the morning see!
   "Sweetheart, rise! Shut out the day!"

Virgin Mary, gentle nurse,
   Patron of lovers, from your throne
Look on us and lend us aid—
   God be with the night that's gone!

Niall MacMurray

Love like heat and cold
　　Pierces and then is gone;
Jealousy when it strikes
　　Sticks in the marrowbone.

The Body's Speech

My grief, my grief, maid without sin,
   Mother of God's Son,
Because of one I cannot win
   My peace is gone.

Mortal love, a raging flood,
   O Mother Maid,
Runs like a fever through my blood,
   Ruins heart and head.

How can I tell her of my fear,
   My wild desire,
When words I speak for my own ear
   Turn me to fire?

I dream of breasts so lilylike,
   Without a fleck,
And hair that, bundled up from her back,
   Burdens her neck.

And praise the cheeks where flames arise
   That shame the rose,
And the soft hands at whose touch flees
   All my repose.

Since I have seen her I am lost,
   A man possessed,
Better to feel the world gone past,
   Earth on my breast;

And from my tomb to hear the choir,
   The hum of prayer;
Without her while her place is here,
   My peace is there.

I am a ghost upon your path,
    A wasting death,
But you must know one word of truth
    Gives a ghost breath—

In language beyond learning's touch
    Passion can teach—
Speak in that speech beyond reproach
    The body's speech.

Donal MacCarthy, First Earl Clancarty

To the Lady with a Book

Pleasant journey, little book
    To that gay gold foolish head!
Though I wish that you remained
    And I travelled in your stead.

Gentle book, 'tis well for you,
    Hastening where my darling rests;
You will see the crimson lips,
    You will touch the throbbing breasts.

You will see the dear grey eye.
    On you will that hand alight—
Ah, my grief 'tis you not I
    Will rest beside her warm at night.

You will see the slender brows
    And the white nape's candle-gleam,
And the fond flickering cheeks of youth
    That I saw last night in dream.

And the waist my arms would clasp
    And the long legs and stately feet
That pace between my sleep and me
    With their magic you will meet.

And the soft pensive sleepy voice
    Whose echoes murmur in my brain
Will bring you rest—'tis well for you!
    When shall I hear that voice again?

The Student

The Irish are a pious race, and the anthology of Irish verse in which I first read this poem makes the fourth verse end "In lovemaking with a friend around him." The Irish is execrable, but the sentiment is of great distinction.

The student's life is pleasant,
    And pleasant is his labour,
Search all Ireland over
    You'll find no better neighbour.

Nor lords nor petty princes
    Dispute the student's pleasure
Nor chapter stints his purse,
    Nor stewardship his leisure.

None orders early rising,
    Calf-rearing or cow-tending,
Nor nights of toilsome vigil;
    His time's his own for spending.

He takes a hand at draughts
    And plucks a harp-string bravely,
And fills his nights with courting
    Some golden-haired light lady.

And when spring-time is come
    The plough-shaft's there to follow—
A fistful of goose-quills
    And a straight, deep furrow.

The Harper

Master of discords John
    Makes harmony seem wrong,
His treble sings to his bass
    Like a sow consoling her young.

If he played with his shoulder-blades
    'Twould yield a pleasanter tone,
He reaches out for a chord
    As a dog snaps at a bone.

Playing away to himself
    God only knows what tune,
Even the man who made it
    Cannot recall his own.

A wonder the way he works
    He never keeps tune or time,
With skill and care he goes wrong,
    Mountains of error climb.

Give him the simplest catch
    And at once you're in at the kill,
He mangles it patiently
    Like an old loud derelict mill.

Copper scratched with a knife,
    Brass cut with a rasp,
His nails scrape at the strings
    Till all shudder and gasp.

God help you gentle harp
    Pounded and plagued by his fist,
There isn't a chord in your breast
    Without a sprain or twist.

The Liar

The manuscript of this poem originally revealed the name of the liar, which contained the letters s, m, p, a, and t, but he has so far escaped further immortality. Mananaun's swine could be endlessly killed and came endlessly to life again.

O you liar tell me this
       How can anyone repay
When he cannot even count
       All the lies you give away?

Many and many a poor man turns
       Empty from your neighbours' doors;
Praise the Lord who keeps you rich,
       All men get their fill at yours.

For you suffer no decrease—
       Such is liars' luck they say;
And you never had a lie
       But you gave the lie away.

And since what you give you keep,
       No whit poorer when 'tis gone,
Woe to him who after you
       Puts a bridle on his tongue.

Curse on any stingy wretch
       Who would keep a falsehood in
Since the yarn you spun last night
       Once again tonight you spin.

Now I know the poet meant
       That the swine of Mananaun
Were the lies killed overnight
       Rising from the dead with dawn.

Showing Off

Girl of three cows don't crow!
    Not so much of your store!
I tell you I used to know
    A girl who had several more.

Wealth is a broken reed,
    If you must brag speak low,
Death's at your back, give heed!
    Girl of three cows don't crow!

MacCarthy had stock enough
    Where did his own stock go?
All its glory a puff.
    Girl of three cows don't crow!

Lord Clare's heroic race
    Passed on a day of woe
No more to be seen it its place—
    Girl of three cows don't crow!

Over the seas in Spain,
    Fighting a foreign foe,
O'Sullivan Beare was slain—
    Girl of three cows don't crow!

The O'Carrolls too were strong
    And brought down every foe,
But poor they have been for long—
    Girl of three cows don't crow!

Of course we know that it's true,
    But you mustn't make such a show
Just for a cow or two—
    Girl of three cows don't crow!

Inheritance

"And what is the new kingdom he inherits? Creeping things and carrion beast, and worm." This verse from Ecclesiasticus the people of the Middle Ages interpreted more particularly.

Three things seek my death,
　　　Hard at my heels they run—
Hang them, sweet Christ, all three,
　　　Devil, maggot and son.

Each of them only craves
　　　The morsel that falls to his share,
And cares not a thrauneen what
　　　Falls to the other pair.

The spirit of guilt and guile
　　　Would compound for my soul in sin
And leave my flesh to the worm,
　　　My money to my kin.

My sons think more of the gold
　　　That will come to them when I die
Than a soul they could not spend
　　　A body that none would buy.

And how would the maggot fare
　　　On a soul too thin to eat
And money too tough to chew?
　　　He must have my body for meat.

Christ speared by the blind man,
　　　Christ nailed to a naked tree,
The three that seek my end,
　　　Hang them, sweet Christ, all three.

Childless

These verses are from a long poem by one of the thir-teenth-century court poets, known as "the Scotchman." As O'Rahilly points out, in spite of the passion of such an intimate poem, he addresses God as though He were a member of the Irish aristocracy with recognized social obligations toward him.

Blessed Trinity have pity!
    You can give the blind man sight,
Fill the rocks with waving grasses—
    Give my house a child tonight.

You can bend the woods with blossom,
    What is there you cannot do?
All the branches burst with leafage,
    What's a little child to you?

Trout out of a spawning bubble,
    Bird from shell and yolk of an egg,
Hazel from a hazel berry—
    Jesus, for a son I beg!

Corn from shoot and oak from acorn
    Miracles of life awake,
Harvest from a fist of seedlings—
    Is a child so hard to make?

Childless men although they prosper
    Are praised only when they are up,
Sterile grace however lovely
    Is a seed that yields no crop.

There is no hell, no lasting torment
    But to be childless at the end,
A naked stone in grassy places,
    A man who leaves no love behind.

God I ask for two things only,
    Heaven when my life is done,
Payment as befits a poet—
    For my poem pay a son.

Plead with Him O Mother Mary,
    Let Him grant the child I crave,
Womb that spun God's human tissue,
    I no human issue leave.

Brigid after whom they named me,
    Beg a son for my reward,
Let no poet empty-handed
    Leave the dwelling of his lord.

Giollabhrighde Mac Conmidhe

Six!
> Such different minds and faces!
Three plagues as false as vicious,
> Three that were only lightness.

Hardship,
> The fishwife left me shattered;
Her giant hooves of iron
> Have left their mark upon me.

Love
> Deludes all creation;
I loved her more than life
> But cannot recall her features.

Gentleness—
> There goes the girl for marriage!
Choice never went beyond her,
> Better than any dowry.

Necessity
> Was sour from the beginning,
The sturdiest woman living,
> Impossible to discipline.

Courage,
> Stately and stern—a beauty!
Though she and I were lovers
> This year past she has shunned men.

Sorrow,
> The one who wears the mourning,
I never liked; officious
> But nonetheless important.

To a Boy

Do not waste your time
    But serve some noble end;
The basketmaker breaks
    The spray that will not bend.

Open your mind in youth
    And let all learning in
For words the head has not shaped
    Are worthless, out and in.

Words not salted with sense,
    Where judgment has no part
Are only a puppy's yelp
    Nearer the lips than the heart.

So let all learning in;
    Be pure in mind and breast
For the voice that speaks to the heart
    Pleases the Master best.

Fathers and Sons

1

Young at his father's fire
    He lords it and takes the best;
Old, at the fire of his son,
    He covers his knees with his breast.

2

Father and son take shares?
    The son the father devours!
All that is ours is theirs,
    Nothing of theirs is ours.

Hugh Maguire

We have seen in the poem on Carroll's sword, court poetry as it was in the ninth century. This is court poetry as it was about the beginning of the seventeenth. Maguire, one of the lieutenants of Hugh O'Neill, the great Earl of Tyrone, was lord of Fermanagh about the year 1600. This was written when he was on a winter campaign in Cork.

Too cold this night for Hugh Maguire,
I tremble at the pounding rain;
 Alas that venomous cold
 Is my companion's lot.

It is an anguish to my heart
To see the fiery torrents fall;
 He and the spiky frost,
 A horror to the mind.

The floodgates of the heavens yawn
Above the bosom of the clouds,
 And every pool a sea
 And murder in the air.

One thinks of the hare that haunts the wood
And of the salmon in the bay,
 Even the wild bird, one grieves
 To think they are abroad.

Then one remembers Hugh Maguire
Abroad in a strange land tonight
 Under the lightning's glare
 And clouds with fury filled.

He in West Munster braves his doom
And without shelter strides between
    The drenched and shivering grass
    And the impetuous sky.

Cold on that tender blushing cheek
The fury of the springtime gales
    That toss the stormy rays
    Of stars about his head.

I can scarce bear to conjure up
The contour of his body crushed
    This rough and gloomy night
    In its cold iron suit.

The gentle and war-mastering hand
To the slim shaft of his cold spear
    By icy weather pinned—
    Cold is this night for Hugh.

The low banks of the swollen streams
Are flooded where the soldiers pass,
    The meadows stiff with ice,
    The horses cannot feed.

And yet as though to bring him warmth
And coax the brightness to his face
    Each wall that he attacks
    Sinks in a wave of fire.

The fury of the fire dissolves
The frost that sheaths the tranquil eye,
    And from his wrists the flame
    Thaws manacles of ice.

Eochy O'Hussey

To Tomas Costello at the Wars

*This mysterious and lovely poem has a history of mis-
understanding behind it. The original editors assumed
that Costello was making love to O'Rourke's wife while
her husband was away at the wars. My translation cor-
rected this misunderstanding by making it clear that it
was Costello who was at the wars, and that his omni-
presence was to be attributed to her imagination rather
than to his obtrusiveness, but the theory of a younger
scholar than Bergin and Gwynn, Mr. Carney, showed
that I had only gone part of the way, for he suggests
that there is no O'Rourke, and that O'Rourke's wife is
a bardic conceit for Ireland. There is no doubt in my
mind that, whether Mr. Carney is right in every partic-
ular or not, this is the only sort of explanation that is
possible. What is astonishing is that court poetry of such
an elaborate kind should have continued to be written
right up to the end of the seventeenth century, and (if
Mr. Carney's attribution to O'Higgins is correct) by one
of the great families of court poets. Even stranger to my
mind is to find court poetry with all the emotionalism
of Baroque, though MacCawell's poem on the Nativity
has something of the same kind.*

*Tomas Costello, known as "Strong Thomas," has be-
come folklore in the West of Ireland. He is supposed to
have had a tragic love affair with a girl called Una
MacDermott, and his lament for Una (if it is his), with
its agonised and blasphemous imagery and its wonderful
melody, makes it the greatest of Irish songs. I am told
that Wolf-Ferrari uses it in one of his operas, but I
have not checked this statement. It seems to me untrans-
latable, but perhaps a verse of it translated into plain
prose may give some idea of its quality.*

84

Young Una, you were a rose in a garden,
You were a gold candlestick on the queen's table,
You were talk and music going before me along the
  road,
My ruin of a sad morning that I was not married
  to you.

Popular rhythms had come in at the time. There is
nothing popular about the rhythms of this poem.

Here's pretty conduct, Hugh O'Rourke,
    Great son of Brian, blossoming bough,
Noblest son of noblest kin,
    What do you say of Costello now?

If you are still the man I loved
    Hurry and aid me while you can,
Do you not see him at my side,
    A walking ghost? What ails you, man?

Brian's son, goal of my song,
    If any thought of losing me
Grieve you, strong pillar of my love,
    Beseech this man to let me be.

Yet there's such darkness in his ways
    Though he a thousand oaths repeat
You must not on your life believe
    But he will try to have me yet.

And if the river of my shame
    He ford but once, that frontier crossed,
You will not rule the land again,
    Past choice of mine my heart is lost.

Fearsome the forms he courts me in,
     Myriad and strange the arts he plies,
Desire, enchantment of the sight,
     Never dons twice the same disguise.

Sometimes I turn and there he stands,
     An unfledged stripling, bashful-eyed,
And swift as ever hawk can swoop
     The heart he snatches from my side.

Or as if I were a whore he comes,
     A young blood curious of my flame,
With sensual magic and dark rhymes
     To woo and mock me in my shame.

Far to the Ulster wars he flies,
     Some town he sacks—I am the town—
With some light love he charms the night—
     Beguiling her, he brings me down.

Sometimes he comes into my room
     So much like you in voice and shape
I am in his arms before I know
     Who holds me—how can I escape?

But when he comes in his own form,
     With his own voice, I stand transfixed;
My love deserts its wonted place,
     My mind no longer holds it fixed.

Dearest, unless you pity me
     And keep my wavering fancy set
And drive that phantom from my side
     I swear that he will have me yet.

I cannot tear myself in two,
    My love, your love within my mind
Pants like a bird within a cage—
    My lover, must you be unkind?

If 'tis not wasted time to plead
    Dear son of Jordans, let me be!
The women of the world are yours,
    I am my husband's, let me be.

O sunmist of the summer's day,
    You will find I am no easy game,
No graceless, love-sick, moony girl,
    I am not dazzled by a name.

Forget the things the neighbours say,
    I am no harlot as you think;
I was a girl when first I loved,
    I have not strayed, you must not wink.

The enchantment of desire is vain,
    I see through every mask you don.
You rascal, pity my good name,
    You thief of laughter, get you gone!

You bandit of the heart, away!
    I shall not give your lust release,
Smother the frontier posts in flame,
    But let my foolish heart in peace.

Bright blossom of the scented wood,
    Yellow Jordans' hope and pride,
For love, for money, or for rank
    I cannot leave my husband's side.

And since I never will be yours
    Take up your father's trade anew,
Go magnify the northern blood—
    The light of poetry are you.

The stirring of the coals of love,
    The voice with which old griefs are healed,
The mast of the rolling sail of war—
    I may be yours, I shall not yield.

And yet, and yet, when all is said,
    All my scolding seems untrue,
My mind to each rebuke replies
    If love I must I must love you.

And now God bless you and begone,
    The time has come for you to go,
For all the grief of parting, I
    Could never grieve my husband so.

Silence, my darling! This is he!
    Go now, although my heart should crack!
Silence! Begone! What shall I do?
    My love! Oh, God! Do not look back!

                Tomas O'Higgins, circa 1680

Christmas Night

Another aspect of Ireland in the late sixteenth century is provided by this poem by the Archbishop of Armagh, tutor to Tyrone's sons. Not only does Irish poetry mark the change from mediaeval to Renaissance; it also marks the change from Renaissance to Baroque. This could have been by Crashaw.

Welcome to us Holy Child
    Though the manger by your bed,
Still in glory of your house
    Happy, happy rests your head.

Child so young and yet so old,
    Child so tiny and so tall,
To a manger that's too wide
    From the skies that were too small.

Motherless through all the years,
    Fatherless upon the earth,
God before the world began,
    As a man you come to birth.

Though your father is so old
    He is but one age with you,
And your mother but a child,
    Older she, but younger too.

With omnipotence that spreads
    To subdue the farthest spheres,
Youngest, oldest, Mercy's child,
    How can we understand your tears?

In a swaddling cloth you lie
   Whom all stars in heaven obey,
You who made the elements
   Weep yourself, new-made of clay.

Virgin, your mother gave you birth,
   She the daughter of her son,
In the blackness of her womb
   Light that knows no setting shone.

Maker of the world made flesh,
   Immortal made mortality—
The time has come for me to speak
   For God, being weak, can only cry.

So silence, lips, and sense be still,
   Reason admit what here is done,
For none shall ever understand
   But Godhead's self the godhead's son.

So welcome Jesus once again!
   Welcome from the Virgin's womb,
Little face that shames the sun,
   Baby God, a welcome home.

Brother, let me kiss your mouth,
   Master, let me kiss your hand
Father, let me kiss your feet,
   There's no more I can demand.

Only mother of my God,
   Open wide the stable door,
And let me as the ox may do
   The master of the skies adore.

I'll be his servant here below,
    And watch for him by night and day,
And from the infant chieftain's side
    Turn the herdboy's dogs away.

I'll wash his poor and ragged clothes,
    And while I dry them in the sun,
O Mary, if you let me I
    Will wrap him warmly in my own.

Hugh MacCawell

Peasants
and
Dreamers

A.D. 1600–A.D. 1800

Patrick Sarsfield, Lord Lucan (circa 1691)

After the siege of Limerick in 1691, Patrick Sarsfield with the flower of the Irish aristocracy passed over to the Continent, where as Catholics they could still achieve positions that matched their birth and rank. A few—like the O'Dwyer of the following poem—lingered, but as little better than outlaws. The O'Connells and O'Learys of a later poem were in fact outlaws. It is astonishing to think that the poem to Tomas Costello and this one really belong to the same period. For the first time we hear the voice of the plain people of Ireland, left without leaders or masters.

Farewell Patrick Sarsfield wherever you may roam,
You crossed the sea to France and left empty camps at home,
To plead our cause before many a foreign throne
Though you left ourselves and poor Ireland overthrown.

Good luck Patrick Sarsfield you were sent to us by God,
And holy forever is the earth that you trod;
May the sun and the white moon light your way,
You trounced King Billy and won the day.

With you Patrick Sarsfield goes the prayer of everyone,
My own prayer too, and the prayer of Mary's Son,
You rode through Birr, the Narrow Ford you passed,
You beat them at Cullen and took Limerick at last.

I'll climb the mountain a lonely man,
And I'll go east again if I can,
'Twas there I saw the Irish ready for the fight,
The lousy crowd that wouldn't unite!

95

Who's that I see now yonder on Howth Head?
"One of Jamie's soldiers sir, now the king has fled,
Last year with gun and knapsack I marched with joyous
    tread,
But this year sir I'm begging my bread."

And God when I think how Diarmuid went under,
His standard broken and his limbs pulled asunder,
And God Himself couldn't fight a way through
When they chopped off his head and held it in our view.

The corn tumbled soon as the scythes went through,
The twelve Kilkenny men were the first that they slew,
My two brothers died and I held my breath,
But the death that broke me was Diarmuid's death.

At the Boyne bridge we took our first beating,
From the bridge at Slane we were soon retreating,
And then we were beaten at Aughrim too—
Ah, fragrant Ireland, that was goodbye to you.

The fumes were choking as the house went alight,
And Black Billy's heroes were warming to the fight,
And every shell that came, wherever it lit,
Colonel Mitchell asked was Lord Lucan hit.

So goodbye Limerick and your homes so fair,
And all the good friends that quartered with us there,
And the cards we played by the watchfires' glare
And the priests that called us all night to prayer.

But on you Londonderry may misfortune come
Like the smoke that lit with every bursting gun
For all the fine soldiers you gathered together
By your walls without shelter from wind or weather.

Many and many a good lad, all proud and gay,
Seven weeks ago they were passing this way,
With guns and swords and pikes on show,
And now in Aughrim they're lying low.

Aughrim has manure that's neither lime nor sand
But sturdy young soldiers to nourish the land,
The men we left behind on the battlefield that day
Torn like horsemeat by the dogs where they lay.

And over the seas are Ireland's best,
The Dukes and the Burkes, Prince Charlie and the rest,
And Captain Talbot their ranks adorning,
And Patrick Sarsfield, Ireland's darling.

Lament for the Woodlands

*In the English clearances after 1691 the woodlands were
the first things to be destroyed because they sheltered the
now landless men of Sarsfield's armies. "The Valley" is
the Glen of Aherlow in Tipperary, and the O'Dwyers
were one of the great Tipperary families.*

When once I rose at morning
The summer sun was shining,
I heard the horn awinding
    With the birds' merry songs;
There was badger and weasel,
Woodcock and plover,
And echo repeated
    The music of the guns.
The winded fox was flying,
The horsemen followed shouting,
Counting her geese on the highway
    Some woman's heart was sore;
But now the woods are falling,
We must go over the water—
Shaun O'Dwyer of the Valley
    Your pleasure is no more.

'Tis cause enough for grieving,
Our shelter felled about us,
The north wind freezing
    And death in the sky,
My merry hound tied tightly
From sporting and chasing
That would lift a young lad's sorrows
    In the noondays gone by.
The stag is on the mountain,
Swift and proud as ever,
He may come up the heather

But our day is o'er,
Let the townsmen cease their watching
And I'll take the ship from Galway,
Shaun O'Dwyer of the Valley
　　Your pleasure is no more.

Kilcash

The same theme, but to a gentler tune. Kilcash was the
home of one branch of the Butler family. Although I
don't think Yeats, who had Butler blood in him, knew
this, it was one of his favourite poems, and there is a
good deal of his work in it.

What shall we do for timber?
    The last of the woods is down.
Kilcash and the house of its glory
    And the bell of the house are gone,
The spot where that lady waited
    Who shamed all women for grace
When earls came sailing to greet her
    And Mass was said in the place.

My grief and my affliction
    Your gates are taken away,
Your avenue needs attention,
    Goats in the garden stray.
The courtyard's filled with water
    And the great earls where are they?
The earls, the lady, the people
    Beaten into the clay.

No sound of duck or geese there,
    Hawk's cry or eagle's call,
No humming of the bees there
    That brought honey and wax for all,
Nor even the song of the birds there
    When the sun goes down in the west,
No cuckoo on top of the boughs there,
    Singing the world to rest.

100

There's mist there tumbling from branches,
    Unstirred by night and by day,
And darkness falling from heaven,
    For our fortune has ebbed away,
There's no holly nor hazel nor ash there,
    The pasture's rock and stone,
The crown of the forest has withered,
    And the last of its game is gone.

I beseech of Mary and Jesus
    That the great come home again
With long dances danced in the garden,
    Fiddle music and mirth among men,
That Kilcash the home of our fathers
    Be lifted on high again,
And from that to the deluge of waters
    In bounty and peace remain.

A Grey Eye Weeping

With the breaking of the Treaty of Limerick by the English in 1691 the Irish Catholics descended into a slavery worse than anything experienced by Negroes in the Southern States. (When the Irish came to America, the Negroes called them "White Niggers.") This period is best represented in the few authentic poems of Egan O'Rahilly, a Kerry poet who lived between 1670 and 1726. In this fine poem he approaches, not one of the masters he would have approached fifty years before—the MacCarthys—but Lord Kenmare, one of the new Anglo-Irish gentry. Hence the bitter repetition of the fellow's name. O'Rahilly himself would have considered "Valentine" a ridiculous name for anyone calling himself a gentleman, and as for "Brown," he would as soon have addressed a "Jones" or a "Robinson." O'Rahilly is a snob, but one of the great snobs of literature.

That my old bitter heart was pierced in this black doom,
That foreign devils have made our land a tomb,
That the sun that was Munster's glory has gone down
Has made me a beggar before you, Valentine Brown.

That royal Cashel is bare of house and guest,
That Brian's turreted home is the otter's nest,
That the kings of the land have neither land nor crown
Has made me a beggar before you, Valentine Brown.

Garnish away in the west with its master banned,
Hamburg the refuge of him who has lost his land,
An old grey eye, weeping for lost renown,
Have made me a beggar before you, Valentine Brown.

Egan O'Rahilly

Reverie at Dawn

In this and the famous poem "Brightness of Brightness"
O'Rahilly standardised the Vision poem in which the
poet sees a vision of Ireland as a young woman who
prophesies the return of the Stuarts.

One morning before Titan thought of stirring his feet
    I climbed alone to a hill where the air was kind,
And saw a throng of magical girls go by
    Who had lived to the north in Croghan time out of
    mind.

All over the land from Galway to Cork of the ships
    It seemed a bright enchanted mist came down,
Acorns on oaks and clear cold honey on stones,
    Fruit upon every tree from root to crown.

They lit three candles that shone in the mist like stars
    On a high hill top in Connello and then were gone,
I followed through Thomond the track of the hooded queens
    And asked them the cause of the zeal of their office at
    dawn.

The tall queen Eevul so bright of countenance said
    'The reason we light three candles on every strand
Is to guide the king who will come to us over the sea
    And make us happy and reign in a fortunate land.'

And then so suddenly did I start from my sleep
    They seemed to be true, the words that had been so
    sweet—
It was just that my soul was sick and spent with grief
    One morning before Titan thought of stirring his feet.

Egan O'Rahilly

103

Brightness of Brightness

I have suppressed this early translation for close on thirty years, and reprint it merely to complete the picture of O'Rahilly's poetry. In Irish the poem is pure music, each line beginning with assonantal rhymes on the short vowel "i" (like "mistress" and "bitter"), which gives it the secretive, whispering quality of dresses rustling or of light feet scurrying in the distance.

Brightness of brightness lonely met me where I wandered,
    Crystal of crystal only by her eyes were splendid,
Sweetness of sweetness lightly in her speech she squandered,
    Rose-red and lily-glow brightly in her cheeks con-
        tended.

Ringlet on ringlet flowed tress on tress of yellow flaming
    Hair, and swept the dew that glowed on the grass in
        showers behind her,
Vesture her breasts bore, mirror-bright, oh, mirror-shaming
    That her fairy northern land yielded her from birth to
        bind them.

There she told me, told me as one that might in loving
    languish,
    Told me of his coming, he for whom the crown was
        wreathed,
Told me of their ruin who banished him to utter anguish,
    More too she told me I dare not in my song have
        breathed.

Frenzy of frenzy 'twas that her beauty did not numb me,
    That I neared the royal serf, the vassal queen that
        held me vassal,
Then I called on Mary's Son to shield me, she started
    from me,

And she fled, the lady, a lightning flash to Luachra
    Castle.

Fleetly too I fled in wild flight with body trembling
    Over reefs of rock and sand, bog and shining plain
        and strand, sure
That my feet would find a path to that place of sad assem-
    bling,
    House of houses reared of old in cold dark druid
        grandeur.

There a throng of wild creatures mocked me with elfin
    laughter,
    And a group of mild maidens, tall with twining silken
        tresses,
Bound in bitter bonds they laid me there, and a moment
    after
    See my lady laughing share a pot-bellied clown's ca-
    resses.

Truth of truth I told her in grief that it shamed her
    To see her with a sleek foreign mercenary lover
When the highest peak of Scotland's race already thrice
        had named her,
    And waited in longing for his exile to be over.

When she heard me speak, she wept, but she wept for pride,
    And tears flowed down in streams from cheeks so
        bright and comely,
She sent a watchman with me to lead me to the moutain-
    side—
    Brightness of brightness who met me walking lonely.

Egan O'Rahilly

A Sleepless Night

I have thought long this wild wet night that brought no rest
    Though I have no gold to watch, or horned kine, or
        sheep—
A storm that made the wave cry out has stirred my breast;
    Neither dogfish nor periwinkle was once my meat.

Ah, if the men who knew me were but here tonight
    With their proud company that held me up secure,
Captains of Munster before their great defeat,
    Not long would Corkaguiney see my children poor.

MacCarthy stern and fearless that most upright man,
    MacCarthy of the Lee whose hearth is dark and cold,
MacCarthy of Kanturk and all his kindred gone—
    The heart within me breaks to think their tale is told.

The heart within my breast tonight is wild with grief
    Because, of all the haughty men who ruled this place,
North Munster and South Munster to the wave beneath,
    None lives, and where they lived lives now an alien
        race.

Ah, famous wave you sang the livelong night below;
    Small wonder if the noise set my wits wandering—
I swear if help could ever come to Ireland now
    I'd strangle in your raucous throat that song you sing.

                        Egan O'Rahilly

Last Lines

Because, like himself, O'Rahilly seemed the last voice of feudalism, Yeats used the final line of this poem for one of his own.

I shall not call for help until they coffin me—
    What good for me to call when hope of help is gone?
Princes of Munster who would have heard my cry
    Will not rise from the dead because I am alone.

Mind shudders like a wave in this tempestuous mood,
    My bowels and my heart are pierced and filled with
        pain
To see our lands, our hills, our gentle neighbourhood,
    A plot where any English upstart stakes his claim.

The Shannon and the Liffey and the tuneful Lee,
    The Boyne and the Blackwater a sad music sing,
The waters of the west run red into the sea—
    No matter what be trumps, their knave will beat our
        king.

And I can never cease weeping these useless tears;
    I am a man oppressed, afflicted and undone
Who where he wanders mourning no companion hears
    Only some waterfall that has no cause to mourn.

Now I shall cease, death comes, and I must not delay
    By Laune and Laine and Lee, diminished of their
        pride,
I shall go after the heroes, ay, into the clay—
    My fathers followed theirs before Christ was crucified.

Egan O'Rahilly

Hope

If seven hundred years of history can be summed up in four lines, they are all here.

Life has conquered, the wind has blown away
Alexander, Caesar and all their power and sway;
Tara and Troy have made no longer stay—
Maybe the English too will have their day.

The Lament for Art O'Leary

*Arthur or Art O'Leary, a colonel in the Austrian
army, outlawed and killed in Carriganimma, County
Cork in 1773 for refusing to sell his famous mare to a
Protestant named Morris for £5.0.0. (Catholics were
not permitted by law to possess a horse of greater value
than this), is buried in the ruined abbey of Kilcrea un-
der an epitaph probably composed by his wife, the
author of this lament, and aunt of Daniel O'Connell.*

> *Lo Arthur Leary, generous, handsome, brave,*
> *Slain in his bloom lies in this humble grave.*

*She is said to have followed up his murderers as she
threatened and to have had the soldiers who shot him
transported. Morris himself is supposed to have been shot
in Cork by O'Leary's brother. The curious intervention
of O'Leary's sister in the lament strongly suggests that
she had originally composed a lament for her brother
in which Eileen O'Connell was taunted, and that the
widow seized on this as a theme and developed it into
the fine poem we know. There is a defensive note about
even the opening lines.*

*The members of her family—the O'Connells of Derry-
nane—whom she mentions are her father, Donal, her
brother Connell, who was drowned in 1765, and her sis-
ter Abby, married to another Austrian officer named
O'Sullivan. Abby is the girl who is supposed to have
been the companion of Maria Theresa. Her twin sister,
Maire, also named, was married to a man named
Baldwin in Macroom, who appears to have surrendered
the mare to Morris in order to avoid legal complica-
tions. The markethouse of the first verse is in Macroom,
and the Mill of the penultimate verse is Millstreet,
County Cork.*

My love and my delight,
The day I saw you first
Beside the markethouse
I had eyes for nothing else
And love for none but you.

I left my father's house
And ran away with you,
And that was no bad choice;
You gave me everything.
There were parlours whitened for me
Bedrooms painted for me,
Ovens reddened for me,
Loaves baked for me,
Joints spitted for me,
Beds made for me
To take my ease on flock
Until the milking time
And later if I pleased.

My mind remembers
That bright spring day,
How your hat with its band
Of gold became you,
Your silver-hilted sword,
Your manly right hand,
Your horse on her mettle
And foes around you
Cowed by your air;
For when you rode by
On your white-nosed mare
The English lowered their head before you
Not out of love for you
But hate and fear,

For, sweetheart of my soul,
The English killed you.

My love and my calf
Of the race of the Earls of Antrim
And the Barrys of Eemokilly,
How well a sword became you,
A hat with a band,
A slender foreign shoe
And a suit of yarn
Woven over the water!

My love and my darling
When I go home
The little lad, Conor,
And Fiach the baby
Will surely ask me
Where I left their father,
I'll say with anguish
'Twas in Kilnamartyr;
They will call the father
Who will never answer.

My love and my mate
That I never thought dead
Till your horse came to me
With bridle trailing,
All blood from forehead
To polished saddle
Where you should be,
Either sitting or standing;
I gave one leap to the threshold,
A second to the gate,
A third upon its back.

I clapped my hands,
And off at a gallop;
I never lingered
Till I found you lying
By a little furze-bush
Without pope or bishop
Or priest or cleric
One prayer to whisper
But an old, old woman,
And her cloak about you,
And your blood in torrents—
Art O'Leary—
I did not wipe if off,
I drank it from my palms.

My love and my delight
Stand up now beside me,
And let me lead you home
Until I make a feast,
And I will roast the meat
And send for company
And call the harpers in,
And I shall make your bed
Of soft and snowy sheets
And blankets dark and rough
To warm the beloved limbs
An autumn blast has chilled.

(His sister speaks.)

My little love, my calf,
This is the image
That last night brought me
In Cork all lonely

On my bed sleeping,
That the white courtyard
And the tall mansion
That we two played in
As children had fallen,
Ballingeary withered
And your hounds were silent,
Your birds were songless
While people found you
On the open mountain
Without priest or cleric
But an old, old woman
And her coat about you
When the earth caught you—
Art O'Leary—
And your life-blood stiffened
The white shirt on you.

My love and treasure,
Where is the woman
From Cork of the white sails
To the bridge of Tomey
With her dowry gathered
And cows at pasture
Would sleep alone
The night they waked you?

(His wife replies.)

My darling, do not believe
One word she is saying,
It is a falsehood
That I slept while others
Sat up to wake you—

'Twas no sleep that took me
But the children crying;
They would not rest
Without me beside them.

O people, do not believe
Any lying story!
There is no woman in Ireland
Who had slept beside him
And borne him three children
But would cry out
After Art O'Leary
Who lies dead before me
Since yesterday morning.

Grief on you, Morris!
Heart's blood and bowels' blood!
May your eyes go blind
And your knees be broken!
You killed my darling
And no man in Ireland
Will fire the shot at you.

Destruction pursue you,
Morris the traitor
Who brought death to my husband!
Father of three children—
Two on the hearth
And one in the womb
That I shall not bring forth.

It is my sorrow
That I was not by
When they fired the shots

To catch them in my dress
Or in my heart, who cares?
If you but reached the hills
Rider of the ready hands.

My love and my fortune
'Tis an evil portion
To lay for a giant—
A shroud and a coffin—
For a big-hearted hero
Who fished in the hill-streams
And drank in bright halls
With white-breasted women.

My comfort and my friend,
Master of the bright sword,
'Tis time you left your sleep;
Yonder hangs your whip,
Your horse is at the door,
Follow the lane to the east
Where every bush will bend
And every stream dry up,
And man and woman bow
If things have manners yet
That have them not I fear.

My love and my sweetness,
'Tis not the death of my people,
Donal Mor O'Connell,
Connell who died by drowning,
Or the girl of six and twenty
Who went across the water
To be a queen's companion—
'Tis not all these I speak of

And call in accents broken
But noble Art O'Leary,
Art of hair so golden,
Art of wit and courage,
Art the brown mare's master,
Swept last night to nothing
Here in Carriganimma—
Perish it, name and people!

My love and my treasure,
Though I bring with me
No throng of mourners,
'Tis no shame for me,
For my kinsmen are wrapped in
A sleep beyond waking,
In narrow coffins
Walled up in stone.

Though but for the smallpox,
And the black death,
And the spotted fever,
That host of riders
With bridles shaking
Would wake the echoes,
Coming to your waking,
Art of the white breast.

Could my calls but wake my kindred
In Derrynane beyond the mountains,
Or Capling of the yellow apples,
Many a proud and stately rider,
Many a girl with spotless kerchief,
Would be here before tomorrow,

Shedding tears about your body,
Art O'Leary, once so merry.

My love and my secret,
Your corn is stacked,
Your cows are milking;
On me is the grief
There's no cure for in Munster.
Till Art O'Leary rise
This grief will never yield
That's bruising all my heart
Yet shut up fast in it,
As 'twere in a locked trunk
With the key gone astray,
And rust grown on the wards.

My love and my calf,
Noble Art O'Leary,
Son of Conor, son of Cady,
Son of Lewis O'Leary,
West of the Valley
And east of Greenane
Where berries grow thickly
And nuts crowd on branches
And apples in heaps fall
In their own season;
What wonder to any
If Iveleary lighted
And Ballingeary
And Gougane of the saints
For the smooth-palmed rider,
The unwearying huntsman
That I would see spurring
From Grenagh without halting

When quick hounds had faltered?
My rider of the bright eyes,
What happened you yesterday?
I thought you in my heart,
When I bought you your fine clothes,
A man the world could not slay.

'Tis known to Jesus Christ
Nor cap upon my head,
Nor shift upon my back
Nor shoe upon my foot,
Nor gear in all my house,
Nor bridle for the mare
But I will spend at law;
And I'll go oversea
To plead before the King,
And if the King be deaf
I'll settle things alone
With the black-blooded rogue
That killed my man on me.

Rider of the white palms,
Go in to Baldwin,
And face the schemer,
The bandy-legged monster—
God rot him and his children!
(Wishing no harm to Maire,
Yet of no love for her,
But that my mother's body
Was a bed to her for three seasons
And to me beside her.)

Take my heart's love,
Dark women of the Mill,

For the sharp rhymes ye shed
On the rider of the brown mare.

But cease your weeping now,
Women of the soft, wet eyes
Till Art O'Leary drink
Ere he go to the dark school—
Not to learn music or song
But to prop the earth and the stone.

The Lament for Yellow-haired Donough

*An uneducated Connacht girl, or someone speaking in
her name, writes the classic lament, the poem that would
have been understood in the ninth century as it was in
the nineteenth by Yeats.*

Ye have seen a marvel in this town,
Yellow-haired Donough and he put down;
In place of his hat a little white cap,
In place of his neck-cloth a hempen rope.

I have come all night without my sleep
Like a little lamb in a drove of sheep,
With naked breast and hair awry
Over Yellow-haired Donough to raise my cry.

I wept the first time by the lake shore,
At the foot of your gallows I wept once more;
I wept again with an aching head
Among the English and you stretched dead.

If only I had you among your kin,
The Ballinrobe or the Sligo men,
They would break the gallows and cut you down
And send you safely among your own.

It was not the gallows that was your due
But to go to the barn and thresh the straw,
And guide your plough-team up and down
Till you had painted the green hill brown.

Yellow-haired Donough, I know your case;
I know what brought you to this bad place:
'Twas the drink going round and the pipes alight
And the dew on the fields at the end of night.

Mullane that brought misfortune on,
My little brother was no stroller's son
But a handsome boy who was bold and quick
And could draw sweet sounds from a hurling stick.

Mullane, may a son not share your floor
Nor a daughter ever leave your door;
The table is empty at foot and head
And Yellow-haired Donough is lying dead.

His marriage portion is in the house,
And it is not horses nor sheep nor cows,
But tobacco and pipes and candles lit—
Not grudging any his share of it.

Slievenamon

This song, which has a magical tune, refers to a local insurrection in 1798. It fills in the historical picture of a people now left leaderless and bewildered.

It is my sorrow that this day's troubles
    Poor Irishmen so sore did strike,
Because our tyrants are laughing at us,
    And say they fear neither fork nor pike;
Our Major never came to lead us,
    We had no orders and drifted on
As you'd send a drover with a cow to the fair
    On the sunny side of Slievenamon.

Ross was the place we were defeated,
    There we left many a pikeman dead,
Little children burned to ashes,
    Women in holes and ditches hid.
But I promise you the men that slew them
    We'll meet them yet with pike and gun,
And we'll drive the yeomen in flight before us
    When we pay them back on Slievenamon.

The sturdy Frenchman with ships in order
    Beneath sharp masts is long at sea;
They're always saying they will come to Ireland,
    And they will set the Irish free.
Light as a blackbird on a green bough swinging
    Would be my heart if the French would come—
O the broken ranks and the trumpets ringing
    On the sunny side of Slievenamon!

The Journeyman

The Irish smuggling vessels brought in claret and brought out recruits for the Continental armies, as this song shows.

Oh, never, never more will I go to Cashel
    To auction off my labour,
And sit all day beside a wall
    And chat with friend and neighbour,
While big fat farmers ride up on their horses
    To ask me for the hiring,
With "Come, young man, you've a long road before you!"
    From journey work I'm retiring.

A journeyman my parents left me,
    Depending on my labour,
Though walking the dews in the early morning
    Will soon bring quartan fever,
And so goodbye to scythe and sickle,
    To herding and to mowing,
For I'll put a pike upon my shoulder
    And go where the French are going.

Farewell, farewell to the home of my fathers
    And to our loving country,
And the boys of Coole—in the time of the troubles
    Themselves and I stood sentry,
And soon a poor and lonely wild-goose
    In foreign quarters slaving,
My heart will sink whenever I think
    Of the journeywork I'm leaving.

To the Blacksmith with a Spade

Owen Roe O'Sullivan, having got a girl in trouble and joined the British Army, is supposed to have won his discharge by a poem on Rodney's victory at sea. Socially he is more degraded than O'Rahilly, the irresponsible as a century of wicked laws had fashioned him, but his songs are as popular among Irish-speakers as those of Burns in Scotland. The smith's name is Fitzgerald; hence the reference to the Gherardini and their supposed Greek ancestry.

Make me a handle as straight as the mast of a ship,
    Seumas you clever man, witty and bountiful,
Sprung through the Geraldine lords from the kings of Greece,
    And fix the treadle and send it back to me soon.

Because the spade is the only thing keeping me now—
    And you know that my thirst for knowledge was always deep.
I'll shoulder my traps and make for Galway that night
    To a place where I'm sure of sixpence a day and my keep.

And whenever I'm feeling low at the end of day,
    And the ganger comes round and assures me I'm dodging it well,
I'll drop a few words about Death's adventurous way
    And the wars of the Greeks in Troy, and the kings that fell.

I'll speak of Samson who had great strength and pride,
    And Alexander, the man who was first of men,
And Caesar who took the sway on the Roman side
    And maybe I'll speak of the feats of Achilles then.

Explaining of course how it came to MacTrain to die,
    And Deirdre the beauty who put the whole world
        astray,
And he'll listen and gawk, and not notice an hour go by,
    And so my learning will lift me through the day.

They'll give me my pay in a lump when the harvest's done,
    I'll tuck it away in a knot in my shirt to keep,
And back to the village, singing and mad for fun—
    And I promise I won't spend sixpence until we meet.

For you're a man like myself with an antique thirst,
    So need I say how we'll give the story an end?
We'll shout and rattle our cans the livelong night
    Till there isn't as much as the price of a pint to spend.

                                        Owen O'Sullivan

125

Prayer at Dawn

*After the great early religious poetry, most religious
poetry in Irish seems to me conventional and pietistic.
This strikes me as having the real passion of early Irish
religion behind it.*

I was taught prayer as a child, to bend the knee,
And beat the breast, asking his peace of Christ;
To wake with delight at the first sweet call of the bird
In praise of the Lord God punished and crucified.

Woe for this sleep on me now and my bed not readied at
      dawn!
And I no longer in haste to praise the might of the King,
Beating my breast and bowing my knees with grief
When the first wind wakes the first bird to sing.

When the cock starts suddenly up with a cry,
And fish rise from the bottom to the water's height,
And buried sparks ascend in the morning fire—
Woe, woe for this slumber of yours, O senseless soul!—

O senseless soul! Great is the folly of sleep
When sparks rise from the hoarded flame at dawn,
And boughs are stirred, and leaves are stirred in the wind
And even the birds are singing the Lord God's praise!

Diarmuid O'Shea

Donal Ogue

"Donal Ogue" (Young Dan) is probably the most famous of Irish songs, and as popular in the Scottish Isles as in Connacht.

Donal Ogue, when you cross the water,
Take me with you to be your partner,
And at fair and market you'll be well looked after,
And you can sleep with the Greek king's daughter.

You said you'd meet me, but you were lying,
Beside the sheepfold when the day was dying,
I whistled first, then I started hailing,
But all I heard was the young lambs' wailing.

You said you'd give me—an airy giver!—
A golden ship with masts of silver,
Twelve market towns to be my fortune
And a fine white mansion beside the ocean.

You said you'd give me—'tis you talk lightly!—
Fish-skin gloves that would fit me tightly,
Bird-skin shoes when I went out walking,
And a silken dress would set Ireland talking.

Ah, Donal Ogue, you'd not find me lazy,
Like many a high-born expensive lady;
I'd do your milking and I'd nurse your baby,
And if you were set on I'd back you bravely.

To Lonely Well I wander sighing,
'Tis there I do my fill of crying,
When I see the world but not my charmer
And all his locks the shade of amber.

I saw you first on a Sunday evening
Before the Easter, and I was kneeling.
'Twas about Christ's passion that I was reading,
But my eyes were on you and my own heart bleeding.

My mother said we should not be meeting,
That I should pass and not give you greeting;
'Twas a good time surely she chose for cheating
With the stable bare and the horse retreating.

You might as well let him have me, mother,
And every penny you have moreover;
Go beg your bread like any other
But him and me don't seek to bother.

Black as a sloe is the heart inside me,
Black as a coal with the griefs that drive me,
Black as a boot print on shining hallways,
And 'twas you that blackened it ever and always.

For you took what's before me and what's behind me,
You took east and west when you wouldn't mind me,
Sun and moon from my sky you've taken,
And God as well, or I'm much mistaken.

Lad of the Curly Locks

Lad of the curly locks
    Who used to be once my darling,
You passed the house last night
    And never bothered calling.
Little enough 'twould harm you
    To comfort me and I crying,
When a single kiss from you
    Would save me and I dying.

If only I had the means
    'Tis little I'd think of giving
To make a lane of my own
    To the place where my lad is living,
Trusting in God that I'd hear
    The sound of his hasty paces,
For I'm many a night awake,
    Longing for his embraces.

I thought you were sun and moon
    When first I met you, my darling,
And then you seemed to me
    Like snow on the hills at morning,
And after that I was sure
    You were God's own lantern swaying
Or the North Star over my head
    To keep my foot from straying.

You said I'd have shawls and shoes,
    Satin and silk hereafter,
And said if I went away
    You'd follow me through the water,
But now an old bush in a gap
    Is all that you are leaving,
As I mind my father's house
    At morning and at evening.

The Orphan

My father and my mother died and left me young and
    poor,
  But I would never mind bad luck if I had my good
    name;
What sort of comfort in this world or mercy at the end
  Can any hope for, having brought the like of me to
    shame?

By the mountain's edge he lives who put my wits astray,
  The laughter on his cheek and his gold hair blown
    behind;
He said he'd marry me, he said my mouth was like a rose—
  How can I see the path for the tears that make me
    blind?

Meadow lands and ploughed lands lie in valleys far away
  Where apple-trees and sloe-bushes grow thickly as at
    home;
If my love say nothing, what matter what all say?
  And if your mother slight me, her blood on the
    hearthstone!

How Well for the Birds

This version of "How Well for the Birds" was collected by a friend of mine who offered a prize of sixpence to some school-children for the best poem they could collect in their own homes. This won the sixpence!

How well for the birds that can rise in their flight
And settle together on the one bough at night,
It is not so with me and the boy of my heart,
Each morning the sun finds us rising apart.

How well for the flowers when my sweetheart goes walking,
How well for the house when he sits in it talking,
How well for the woman with whom he'll be sleeping,
Her morning star and her star of evening.

As white as the sloebush in spring is my darling,
As bright as the seabirds from wave to wave swarming,
As the sun fills the ocean all day with its gleaming,
Rising and setting he fills all my dreaming.

County Mayo

The gentle maunderings of Anthony Raftery one of the last of the folk poets, are as close as genuine poetry has ever approached to doggerel. The magnificent reply to someone who asked who the blind man playing the fiddle was is literature.

> *I am Raftery the poet,*
> *Full of hope and love,*
> *With sightless eyes*
> *And undistracted calm.*
>
> *Going west on my journey*
> *By the light of my heart,*
> *Weak and tired*
> *To the end of my road.*
>
> *Look at me now!*
> *My face to the wall,*
> *Playing music*
> *To empty pockets.*

Not, just the same, the sort of literature Raftery wrote.

Now with the springtime the days will grow longer,
    And after St. Bride's Day my sail I'll let go;
I put my mind to it and I never will linger
    Till I find myself back in the County Mayo.
It is in Claremorris I'll stop the first evening;
    At Balla beneath it I'll first take the floor;
I'll go to Kiltimagh and have a month's peace there,
    And that's not two miles from Ballinamore.

I give you my word that the heart in me rises
    As when the wind rises and all the mists go,

Thinking of Carra and Gallen beneath it,
    Scahaveela and all the wide plains of Mayo;
Killeadan's the village where everything pleases,
    Of berries and all sorts of fruit there's no lack,
And if I could but stand in the heart of my people
    Old age would drop from me and youth would come
    back.

Anthony Raftery

Mary Hynes

*This song has the same sort of wailful charm: a blind
man praising a village beauty whom he cannot see.*

Going to Mass by the heavenly mercy,
    The day was rainy, the wind was wild;
I met a lady beside Kiltartan
    And fell in love with the lovely child;
My conversation was smooth and easy,
    And graciously she answered me
"Raftery dear, 'tis yourself that's welcome,
    So step beside me to Ballylee."

This invitation there was no denying,
    I laughed with joy and my poor heart beat;
We had but to walk across a meadow,
    And in her dwelling I took my seat.
There was laid a table with a jug and glasses,
    And that sweet maiden sat down by me—
"Raftery drink and don't spare the liquor;
    There's a lengthy cellar in Ballylee."

If I should travel France and England,
    And Spain and Greece and return once more
To study Ireland to the northern ocean,
    I would find no morsel the like of her.
If I was married to that youthful beauty
    I'd follow her through the open sea,
And wander coasts and winding roads
    With the shining pearl of Ballylee.

'Tis fine and bright on the mountainside,
    Looking down on Ballylee,
You can walk the woods, picking nuts and berries,
    And hear the birds sing merrily;

But where's the good if you got no tidings
    Of the flowering branch that resides below—
O summer sky, there's no denying
    It is for you that I ramble so.

My star of beauty, my sun of autumn,
    My golden hair, O my share of life!
Will you come with me this coming Sunday
    And tell the priest you will be my wife?
I'd not grudge you music, nor a feast at evening,
    Nor punch nor wine, if you'd have it be,
And King of Glory, dry up the roadway
    Till I find my posy at Ballylee!

Anthony Raftery

The Midnight Court

I like to walk in the river meadows
In the thick of the dew and the morning shadows,
At the edge of the woods in a deep defile
At peace with myself in the first sunshine.
When I looked at Lough Graney my heart grew bright,
Ploughed lands and green in the morning light,
Mountains in rows with crimson borders
Peering above their neighbours' shoulders.
The heart that never had known relief
In a lonesome old man distraught with grief,
Without money or home or friends or ease,
Would quicken to glimpse beyond the trees
The ducks sail by on a mistless bay
And a swan before them lead the way;
A speckled trout that in their track
Splashed in the air with arching back;
The grey of the lake and the waves around
That foamed at its edge with a hollow sound.
Birds in the trees sang merry and loud;
A fawn flashed out of the shadowy wood;
The horns rang out with the huntsman's cry
And the belling of hounds while the fox slipped by.

Yesterday morning the sky was clear,
The sun fell hot on river and mere,
Its horses fresh and with gamesome eye
Harnessed again to assail the sky;
The leaves were thick upon every bough
And ferns and grass were thick below,
Sheltering bowers of herbs and flowers
That would comfort a man in his dreariest hours.
Longing for sleep bore down my head,
And in the grass I scooped a bed
With a hollow behind to house my back,

A prop for my head and my limbs stretched slack.
What more could one ask? I covered my face
To avert the flies as I dozed a space,
But my mind in dreams was filled with grief
And I tossed and groaned as I sought relief.

I had only begun when I felt a shock,
And all the landscape seemed to rock;
A north wind made my senses tingle
And thunder crackled along the shingle.
As I looked up—as I thought, awake—
I seemed to see at the edge of the lake
As ugly a brute as man could see
In the shape of woman approaching me;
For, if I calculated right,
She must have been twenty feet in height,
With yards and yards of hairy cloak
Trailing behind her in the muck.
There never was seen such a freak of nature;
Without a single presentable feature;
Her grinning jaws with the fangs stuck out
Would be cause sufficient to start a rout,
And in a hand like a weaver's beam
She raised a staff that it might be seen
She was coming on a legal errand,
For nailed to the staff was a bailiff's warrant.

She cried in a voice with a brassy ring:
"Get up out of that, you lazy thing!
That a man like you could think 'tis fitting
To lie in a ditch while the court is sitting!
A decenter court than e'er you knew,
And far too good for the likes of you.
Justice and Mercy hand in hand

Sit in the courts of Fairyland.
Let Ireland think when her trouble's ended
Of those by whom she was befriended.
In Moy Graney palace twelve days and nights
They've sat discussing your wrongs and rights.
All mourned that follow in his train,
Like the king himself, that in his reign
Such unimaginable disaster
Should follow your people, man and master.
Old stock uprooted on every hand
Without claim to rent or law or land;
Nothing to see in a land defiled
Where the flowers were plucked but the weeds and wild;
The best of your breed in foreign places,
And upstart rogues with impudent faces,
Planning with all their guile and spleen
To pick the bones of the Irish clean.
But worst of all those bad reports
Was that truth was darkened in their courts,
And nothing to back a poor man's case
But whispers, intrigue and the lust for place;
The lawyer's craft and the rich man's might,
Cozening, favour, greed and spite;
Maddened with jobs and bribes and malice,
Anarchy loose on cot and palace.

"'Twas all discussed, and along with the rest
There were women in scores who came to attest—
A plea that concerns yourself as well—
That the youth of the country's gone to hell,
And men's increase is a sort of crime,
Which only happened within our time;
Nothing but weeds for want of tillage
Since famine and war assailed the village,

138

And a flighty king and emigration—
And what have you done to restore the nation?
Shame on you without chick nor child
With women in thousands running wild!
The blossoming tree and the young green shoot,
The strap that would sleep with any old root,
The little white saint at the altar rail,
And the proud, cold girl like a ship in sail—
What matter to you if their beauty founder,
If belly and breast will never be rounder,
If, ready and glad to be mother and wife,
They drop unplucked from the boughs of life?

"And having considered all reports,
They agreed that in place of the English courts,
They should select a judge by lot
Who'd hold enquiry on the spot.
Then Eevul, Queen of the Grey Rock,
Who rules all Munster herd and flock,
Arose, and offered to do her share
By putting an end to injustice there.
She took an oath to the council then
To judge the women and the men,
Stand by the poor though all ignore them
And humble the pride of the rich before them;
Make might without right conceal its face
And use her might to give right its place.
Her favour money will not buy,
No lawyer will pull the truth awry,
The smoothest perjurer will not dare
To make a show of falsehood there.
The court is sitting today in Feakle,
So off with you now as quick as you're able!
Come on, I say, and give no back chat,

Or I'll take my stick and knock you flat."
With the crook of her staff she hooked my cape,
And we went at a speed to make Christians gape
Away through the glens in one wild rush
Till we stood in Moinmoy by the ruined church.

Then I saw with an awesome feeling
A building aglow from floor to ceiling,
Lighted within by guttering torches
Among massive walls and echoing arches.
The Queen of the Fairies sat alone
At the end of the hall on a gilded throne,
While keeping back the thronged beholders
Was a great array of guns and soldiers.
I stared at it all, the lighted hall,
Crammed with faces from wall to wall,
And a young woman with downcast eye,
Attractive, good-looking and shy,
With long and sweeping golden locks
Who was standing alone in the witness box.
The cut of her spoke of some disgrace;
I saw misfortune in her face;
Her tearful eyes were red and hot,
And her passions bubbled as in a pot;
But whatever on earth it was provoked her
She was silent, all but the sobs that choked her.
You could seen from the way the speaking failed her
She'd sooner death than the thing that ailed her,
But, unable to express her meaning,
She wrung her hands and pursued her grieving
While all we could do was stand and gaze
Till sobs gave place to a broken phrase,
And bit by bit she mastered her sorrows,
And dried her eyes, and spoke as follows—

"Yourself is the woman we're glad to see,
Eevul, Queen of Carriglee,
Our moon at night, our morning light,
Our comfort in the teeth of spite;
Mistress of the host of delight,
Munster and Ireland stand in your sight.
My chief complaint and principal grief,
The thing that gives me no relief,
Sweeps me from harbour in my mind
And blows me like smoke on every wind
Is all the girls whose charms miscarry
Throughout the land and who'll never marry;
Bitter old maids without house or home,
Put on one side through no fault of their own.
I know myself from the things I've seen
Enough and to spare of the sort I mean,
And to give an example, here am I
While the tide is flowing, left high and dry.
Wouldn't you think I must be a fright,
To be shelved before I get started right;
Heartsick, bitter, dour and wan,
Unable to sleep for the want of a man?
But how can I lie in a lukewarm bed
With all the thoughts that come into my head?
Indeed, 'tis time that somebody stated
The way that the women are situated,
For if men go on their path to destruction
There will nothing be left to us but abduction.
Their appetite wakes with age and blindness
When you'd let them cover you only from kindness,
And offer it up for the wrongs you'd done
In hopes of reward in the life to come:
And if one of them weds in the heat of youth
When the first down is on his mouth

141

It isn't some woman of his own sort,
Well-shaped, well-mannered or well-taught;
Some mettlesome girl who studied behavior,
To sit and stand and amuse a neighbour,
But some pious old prude or dour defamer
Who sweated the couple of pounds that shame her.
There you have it! It has me melted,
And makes me feel that the world's demented:
A county's choice for brains and muscle,
Fond of a lark and not scared of a tussle,
Decent and merry and sober and steady,
Good-looking, gamesome, rakish and ready;
A boy in the blush of his youthful vigour
With a gracious flush and a passable figure
Finds a fortune the best attraction
And sires himself off on some bitter extraction;
Some fretful old maid with her heels in the dung,
Pious airs and venomous tongue,
Vicious and envious, nagging and whining,
Snoozing and snivelling, plotting, contriving—
Hell to her soul, an unmannerly sow
With a pair of bow legs and hair like tow
Went off this morning to the altar
And here am I still without hope of the halter!
Couldn't some man love me as well?
Amn't I plump and sound as a bell?
Lips for kissing and teeth for smiling,
Blossomy skin and forehead shining?
My eyes are blue and my hair is thick
And coils in streams about my neck—
A man who's looking for a wife,
Here's a face that will keep for life!
Hand and arm and neck and breast,
Each is better than the rest.

142

Look at that waist! My legs are long,
Limber as willows and light and strong.
There's bottom and belly that claim attention,
And the best concealed that I needn't mention.
I'm the sort a natural man desires,
Not a freak or a death-on-wires,
A sloven that comes to life in flashes,
A creature of moods with her heels in the ashes,
Or a sluggard stewing in her own grease,
But a good-looking girl that's bound to please.
If I was as slow as some I know
To stand up for my rights and my dress a show,
Some brainless, illbred, country mope
You could understand if I lost hope;
But ask the first you meet by chance:
Hurling match or race or dance,
Pattern or party, market or fair,
Whatever it was, was I not there?
And didn't I make a good impression
Turning up in the height of fashion?
My hair was washed and combed and powdered,
My coif like snow and stiffly laundered;
I'd a little white hood with ribbons and ruff
On a spotted dress of the finest stuff,
And facings to show off the line
Of a cardinal cloak the colour of wine;
A cambric apron filled with showers
Of fruit and birds and trees and flowers;
Neatly-fitting, expensive shoes
With the highest of heels pegged up with screws;
Silken gloves, and myself in spangles
Of brooches, buckles, rings and bangles.
And you mustn't imagine I was shy,
The sort that slinks with a downcast eye,

Solitary, lonesome, cold and wild,
Like a mountainy girl or an only child.
I tossed my cap at the crowds of the races
And kept my head in the toughest places.
Am I not always on the watch
At bonfire, dance or hurling match,
Or outside the chapel after Mass
To coax a smile from fellows that pass?
But I'm wasting my time on a wildgoose-chase,
And my spirit's broken—and that's my case!
After all my shaping, sulks and passions
All my aping of styles and fashions,
All the times that my cards were spread
And my hands were read and my cup was read;
Every old rhyme, pishrogue and rune,
Crescent, full moon and harvest moon,
Whit and All Souls and the First of May,
I've nothing to show for all they say.
Every night when I went to bed
I'd a stocking of apples beneath my head;
I fasted three canonical hours
To try and come round the heavenly powers;
I washed my shift where the stream was deep
To hear a lover's voice in sleep;
Often I swept the woodstack bare,
Burned bits of my frock, my nails, my hair,
Up the chimney stuck the flail,
Slept with a spade without avail;
Hid my wool in the lime-kiln late
And my distaff behind the churchyard gate;
I had flax on the road to halt coach or carriage
And haycocks stuffed with heads of cabbage,
And night and day on the proper occasions
Invoked Old Nick and all his legions;

But 'twas all no good and I'm broken-hearted
For here I'm back at the place I started;
And this is the cause of all my tears
I am fast in the rope of the rushing years,
With age and need in lessening span,
And death beyond, and no hopes of a man.
But whatever misfortunes God may send
May He spare me at least that lonesome end,
Nor leave me at last to cross alone
Without chick nor child when my looks are gone
As an old maid counting the things I lack
Scowling thresholds that warn me back!
God, by the lightning and the thunder,
The thought of it makes me ripe for murder!
Every idiot in the country
With a man of her own has the right to insult me.
Sal' has a slob with a well-stocked farm,
And Molly goes round on a husband's arm,
There's Min and Margery leaping with glee
And never done with their jokes at me.
And the bounce of Sue! and Kitty and Anne
Have children in droves and a proper man,
And all with their kind can mix and mingle
While I go savage and sour and single.

"Now I know in my heart that I've been too quiet
With a remedy there though I scorned to try it
In the matter of draughts and poisonous weeds
And medicine men and darksome deeds
That I know would fetch me a sweetheart plighted
Who'd love me, whether or not invited.
Oh, I see 'tis the thing that most prevails
And I'll give it a trial if all fruit fails—
A powerful aid to the making of splices

Is powdered herbs on apples in slices.
A girl I know had the neighbours yapping
When she caught the best match in the county napping,
And 'twas she that told me under a vow
That from Shrove to All Souls—and she's married now—
She was eating hay like a horse by the pail
With bog-roots burned and stuped in ale—
I've waited too long and was too resigned,
And nothing you say can change my mind;
I'll give you a chance to help me first
And I'm off after that to do my worst."

2

Then up there jumps from a neighbouring chair
A little old man with a spiteful air,
Staggering legs and panting breath,
And a look in his eye like poison and death;
And this apparition stumps up the hall
And says to the girl in the hearing of all:
"Damnation take you, you bastard's bitch,
Got by a tinkerman under a ditch!
No wonder the seasons are all upsot,
Nor every beating Ireland got;
Decline in decency and manners,
And the cows gone dry and the price of bonhams!
Mavrone! what more can we expect
With Doll and Moll and the way they're decked?
You slut of ill-fame, allow your betters
To tell the court how you learned your letters!
Your seed and breed for all your brag
Were tramps to a man with rag and bag;
I knew your da and what passed for his wife,
And he shouldered his traps to the end of his life,

146

An aimless lout without friend or neighbour,
Knowledge or niceness, wit or favour:
The breeches he wore were riddled with holes
And his boots without a tack of the soles.
Believe me, friends, if you sold at a fair,
Himself and his wife, his kids and gear,
When the costs were met, by the Holy Martyr,
You'd still go short for a glass of porter.
But the devil's child has the devil's cheek—
You that never owned cow nor sheep,
With buckles and brogues and rings to order—
You that were reared in the reek of solder!
However the rest of the world is gypped
I knew you when you went half-stripped;
And I'd venture a guess that in what you lack
A shift would still astonish your back;
And, shy as you seem, an inquisitive gent
Might study the same with your full consent.
Bosom and back are tightly laced,
Or is it the stays that gives you the waist?
Oh, all can see the way you shine,
But your looks are no concern of mine.
Now tell us the truth and don't be shy
How long are you eating your dinner dry?
A meal of spuds without butter or milk,
And dirt in layers beneath the silk.
Bragging and gab are yours by right,
But I know too where you sleep at night,
And blanket or quilt you never saw
But a strip of old mat and a bundle of straw,
In a hovel of mud without a seat,
And slime that settles about your feet,
A carpet of weeds from door to wall
And hens inscribing their tracks on all;

The rafters in with a broken back
And brown rain lashing through every crack—
'Twas there you learned to look so nice,
But now may we ask how you came by the price?
We all admired the way you spoke,
But whisper, treasure, who paid for the cloak?
A sparrow with you would die of hunger—
How did you come by all the grandeur,
All the tassles and all the lace—
Would you have us believe they were got in grace?
The frock made a hole in somebody's pocket,
And it wasn't you that paid for the jacket;
But assuming that and the rest no news,
How the hell did you come by the shoes?

"Your worship, 'tis women's sinful pride
And that alone has the world destroyed.
Every young man that's ripe for marriage
Is hooked like this by some tricky baggage,
And no one is secure, for a friend of my own,
As nice a boy as ever I've known
That lives from me only a perch or two—
God help him!—married misfortune too.
It breaks my heart when she passes by
With her saucy looks and head held high,
Cows to pasture and fields of wheat,
And money to spare—and all deceit!
Well-fitted to rear a tinker's clan,
She waggles her hips at every man,
With her brazen face and bullock's hide,
And such airs and graces, and mad with pride.
And—that God may judge me!—only I hate
A scandalous tongue, I could relate
Things of that woman's previous state

As one with whom every man could mate
In any convenient field or gate
As the chance might come to him early or late!
But now, of course, we must all forget
Her galloping days and the pace she set;
The race she ran in Ibrackane,
In Manishmore and Teermaclane,
With young and old of the meanest rabble
Of Ennis, Clareabbey and Quin astraddle!
Toughs from Tradree out on a fling,
And Cratlee cutthroats sure to swing;
But still I'd say 'twas the neighbours' spite,
And the girl did nothing but what was right,
But the devil take her and all she showed!
I found her myself on the public road,
On the naked earth with a bare backside
And a Garus turf-cutter astride!
Is it any wonder my heart is failing,
That I feel that the end of the world is nearing,
When, ploughed and sown to all men's knowledge,
She can manage the child to arrive with marriage,
And even then, put to the pinch,
Begrudges Charity an inch;
For, counting from the final prayer
With the candles quenched and the altar bare
To the day when her offspring takes the air
Is a full nine months with a week to spare?

"But you see the troubles a man takes on!
From the minute he marries his peace is gone;
Forever in fear of a neighbour's sneer—
And my own experience cost me dear.
I lived alone as happy as Larry
Till I took it into my head to marry,

Tilling my fields with an easy mind,
Going wherever I felt inclined,
Welcomed by all as a man of price,
Always ready with good advice.
The neighbours listened—they couldn't refuse
For I'd money and stock to uphold my views—
Everything came at my beck and call
Till a woman appeared and destroyed it all:
A beautiful girl with ripening bosom,
Cheeks as bright as apple-blossom,
Hair that glimmered and foamed in the wind,
And a face that blazed with the light behind;
A tinkling laugh and a modest carriage
And a twinkling eye that was ripe for marriage.
I goggled and gaped like one born mindless
Till I took her face for a form of kindness,
Though that wasn't quite what the Lord intended
For He marked me down like a man offended
For a vengeance that wouldn't be easy mended
With my folly exposed and my comfort ended.

"Not to detain you here all day
I married the girl without more delay,
And took my share in the fun that followed.
There was plenty for all and nothing borrowed.
Be fair to me now! There was no one slighted;
The beggarmen took the road delighted;
The clerk and mummers were elated;
The priest went home with his pocket weighted.
The lamps were lit, the guests arrived;
The supper was ready, the drink was plied;
The fiddles were flayed, and, the night advancing,
The neighbours joined in the sport and dancing.

150

"A pity to God I didn't smother
When first I took the milk from my mother,
Or any day I ever broke bread
Before I brought that woman to bed!
For though everyone talked of her carouses
As a scratching post of the publichouses
That as sure as ever the glasses would jingle
Flattened herself to married and single,
Admitting no modesty to mention,
I never believed but 'twas all invention.
They added, in view of the life she led,
I might take to the roads and beg my bread,
But I took it for talk and hardly minded—
Sure, a man like me could never be blinded!—
And I smiled and nodded and off I tripped
Till my wedding night when I saw her stripped,
And knew too late that this was no libel
Spread in the pub by some jeaous rival—
By God, 'twas a fact, and well-supported:
I was a father before I started!

"So there I was in the cold daylight,
A family man after one short night!
The women around me, scolding, preaching,
The wife in bed and the baby screeching.
I stirred the milk as the kettle boiled
Making a bottle to give the child;
All the old hags at the hob were cooing
As if they believed it was all my doing—
Flattery worse than ever you heard:
'Glory and praise to our blessed Lord,
Though he came in a hurry, the poor little creature,
He's the spit of his da in every feature.

151

Sal, will you look at the cut of that lip!
There's fingers for you! Feel his grip!
Would you measure the legs and the rolls of fat!
Was there ever a seven month child like that?'
And they traced away with great preciseness
My matchless face in the baby's likeness;
The same snub nose and frolicsome air,
And the way I laugh and the way I stare;
And they swore that never from head to toe
Was a child that resembled his father so.
But they wouldn't let me go near the wonder—
'Sure, a draught would blow the poor child asunder!'
All of them out to blind me further—
'The least little breath would be noonday murder!'
Malice and lies! So I took the floor,
Mad with rage and I cursed and swore,
And bade them all to leave my sight.
They shrank away with faces white,
And moaned as they handed me the baby:
'Don't crush him now! Can't you handle him easy?
The least thing hurts them. Treat him kindly!
Some fall she got brought it on untimely.
Don't lift his head but leave him lying!
Poor innocent scrap, and to think he's dying!
If he lives at all till the end of day
Till the priest can come 'tis the most we'll pray!'

"I off with the rags and set him free,
And studied him well as he lay on my knee.
That too, by God, was nothing but lies
For he staggered myself with his kicks and cries.
A pair of shoulders like my own,
Legs like sausages, hair fullgrown;
His ears stuck out and his nails were long,

152

His hands and wrists and elbows strong;
His eyes were bright, his nostrils wide,
And the knee-caps showing beneath his hide—
A champion, begod, a powerful whelp,
As healthy and hearty as myself!

"Young woman, I've made my case entire.
Justice is all that I require.
Once consider the terrible life
We lead from the minute we take a wife,
And you'll find and see that marriage must stop
And the men unmarried must be let off.
And, child of grace, don't think of the race;
Plenty will follow to take our place;
There are ways and means to make lovers agree
Without making a show of men like me.
There's no excuse for all the exploiters;
Cornerboys, clerks and priests and pipers—
Idle fellows that leave you broke
With the jars of malt and the beer they soak,
When the Mother of God herself could breed
Without asking the views of clerk or creed.
Healthy and happy, wholesome and sound,
The come-by-twilight sort abound;
No one assumes but their lungs are ample,
And their hearts as sound as the best example.
When did Nature display unkindness
To the bastard child in disease or blindness?
Are they not handsomer, better-bred
Than many that come of a lawful bed?

"I needn't go far to look for proof
For I've one of the sort beneath my roof—
Let him come here for all to view!

Look at him now! You see 'tis true.
Agreed, we don't know his father's name,
But his mother admires him just the same,
And if in all things else he shines
Who cares for his baptismal lines?
He isn't a dwarf or an old man's error,
A paralytic or walking terror,
He isn't a hunchback or a cripple
But a lightsome, laughing gay young divil.
'Tis easy to see he's no flash in the pan;
No sleepy, good-natured, respectable man,
Without sinew or bone or belly or bust,
Or venom or vice or love or lust,
Buckled and braced in every limb
Spouted the seed that flowered in him:
For back and leg and chest and height
Prove him to all in the teeth of spite
A child begotten in fear and wonder
In the blood's millrace and the body's thunder.

"Down with marriage! It's out of date;
It exhausts the stock and cripples the state.
The priest has failed with whip and blinker
Now give a chance to Tom the Tinker,
And mix and mash in Nature's can
The tinker and the gentleman!
Let lovers in every lane extended
Struggle and strain as God intended
And locked in frenzy bring to birth
The morning glory of the earth;
The starry litter, girl and boy
Who'll see the world once more with joy.
Clouds will break and skies will brighten,
Mountains bloom and spirits lighten,

And men and women praise your might,
You who restore the old delight."

3

The girl had listened without dissembling,
Then up she started, hot and trembling,
And answered him with eyes alight
And a voice that shook with squalls of spite:
"By the Crown of the Rock, I thought in time
Of your age and folly and known decline,
And the manners I owe to people and place
Or I'd dye my nails in your ugly face;
Scatter your guts and tan your hide
And ferry your soul to the other side.
I'd honour you much if I gave the lie
To an impudent speech that needs no reply;
'Tis enough if I tell the sort of life
You led your unfortunate, decent wife.

"This girl was poor, she hadn't a home,
Or a single thing she could call her own,
Drifting about in the saddest of lives,
Doing odd jobs for other men's wives,
As if for drudgery created,
Begging a crust from women she hated.
He pretended her troubles were over;
Married to him she'd live in clover;
The cows she milked would be her own,
The feather bed and the decent home,
The stack of turf, the lamp to light,
The good earth wall of a winter's night,
Flax and wool to weave and wind,
The womanly things for which she pined.

Even his friends could not have said
That his looks were such that she lost her head.
How else would he come by such a wife
But that ease was the alms she asked of life?
What possible use could she have at night
For dourness, dropsy, bother and blight,
A basket of bones with thighs of lead,
Knees absconded from the dead,
Fire-speckled shanks and temples whitening,
Looking like one that was struck by lightning?
Is there living a girl who could grow fat
Tied to a travelling corpse like that
Who twice a year wouldn't find a wish
To see what was she, flesh or fish
But dragged the clothes about his head
Like a wintry wind to a woman in bed?

"Now was it too much to expect as right
A little attention once a night?
From all I know she was never accounted
A woman too modest to be mounted.
Gentle, good-humoured and Godfearing
Why should we think she'd deny her rearing?
Whatever the lengths his fancy ran
She wouldn't take fright from a mettlesome man,
And would sooner a boy would be aged a score
Than himself on the job for a week or more;
And an allnight dance or Mass at morning,
Fiddle or flute or choir or organ,
She'd sooner the tune that boy would play
As midnight struck or at break of day.
Damn it, you know we're all the same,
A woman nine months in terror and pain,
The minute that Death has lost the game—

Good morrow my love, and she's off again!
And how could one who longed to please
Feel with a fellow who'd sooner freeze
Than warm himself in a natural way
From All Souls Night to St. Brigid's day?
You'd all agree 'twas a terrible fate—
Sixty winters on his pate,
A starved old gelding, blind and lamed
And a twenty year old with her parts untamed.
It wasn't her fault if things went wrong,
She closed her eyes and held her tongue;
She was no ignorant girl from school
To whine for her mother and play the fool
But a competent bedmate smooth and warm
Who cushioned him like a sheaf of corn.
Line by line she bade him linger
With gummy lips and groping finger,
Gripping his thighs in a wild embrace
Rubbing her brush from knee to waist
Stripping him bare to the cold night air,
Everything done with love and care.
But she'd nothing to show for all her labour;
There wasn't a jump in the old deceiver,
And all I could say would give no notion
Of that poor distracted girl's emotion,
Her knees cocked up and the bedposts shaking,
Chattering teeth and sinews aching,
While she sobbed and tossed through a joyless night
And gave it up with the morning light.

"I think you'll agree from the little I've said
A man like this must be off his head
To live like a monk to the end of his life
Muddle his marriage and blame his wife.

The talk about women comes well from him,
Without hope in body or help in limb;
If the creature that found him such a sell
Has a lover today she deserves him well:
A benefit Nature never denies
To anything born that swims or flies;
Tell me of one that ever went empty
And died of want in the midst of plenty.
In all the wonders west and east
Where will you hear of a breed of beast
That will turn away from fern and hay
To feed on briars and roots and clay?
You silly old fool, you can't reply
And give us at least one reason why
If your supper is there when you come back late
You've such talk of someone that used the plate.
Will it lessen your store, will you sigh for more
If twenty millions cleaned it before?
You must think that women are all like you
To believe they'll go dry for a man or two;
You might as well drink the ocean up
Or empty the Shannon with a cup.
Ah, you must see that you're half insane;
Try cold compresses, avoid all strain,
And stop complaining about the neighbours,
If every one of them owed her favours,
Men by the hundred beneath her shawl
Would take nothing from you in the heel of all.

"If your jealousy even was based on fact
In some hardy young whelp that could keep her packed;
Covetous, quarrelsome, keen on scoring,
Or some hairy old villain hardened with whoring;
A vigorous pusher, a rank outsider,

A jockey of note or a gentleman rider—
But a man disposed in the wrong direction
With a poor mouth shown on a sham erection!

"But oye, my heart will grow grey hairs
Brooding forever on idle cares,
Has the Catholic Church a glimmer of sense
That the priests won't come to the girls' defense?
Is it any wonder the way I moan,
Out of my mind for a man of my own
While there's men around can afford one well
But shun a girl as they shun Hell.
The full of a fair of primest beef,
Warranted to afford relief;
Cherry-red cheeks and bull-like voices
And bellies dripping with fat in slices;
Backs erect and huge hind-quarters,
Hot-blooded men, the best of partners,
Freshness and charm, youth and good looks
And nothing to ease their mind but books!
The best-fed men that travel the country,
With beef and mutton, game and poultry,
Whiskey and wine forever in stock,
Sides of bacon and beds of flock.
Mostly they're hardy under the hood,
And we know like ourselves they're flesh and blood.
I wouldn't ask much of the old campaigners,
Good-for-nothings and born complainers
But petticoat-tossers aloof and idle
And fillies gone wild for bit and bridle!

"Of course I admit that some, more sprightly,
Would like to repent, and I'd treat them lightly.
A pardon and a job for life

To every priest that takes a wife!
For many a good man's chance miscarries
If you scuttle the ship for the crooks it carries;
And though some as we know were always savage,
Gnashing their teeth at the thought of marriage,
And, modest beyond the needs of merit,
Invoked hell-fire on girls of spirit,
Yet some who took to their pastoral labours
Made very good priests and the best of neighbours.
Many a girl filled byre and stall
And furnished her house through a clerical call.
Everyone's heard some priest extolled
For the lonesome women that he consoled;
People I've known throughout the county
Have nothing but praise for the curate's bounty,
Or uphold the canon to lasting fame
For the children he reared in another man's name;
But I hate to think of their lonely lives,
The passions they waste on middle-aged wives
While the girls they'd choose if the choice was theirs
Go by the wall and comb grey hairs.

"I leave it to you, O Nut of Knowledge,
The girls at home and the boys in college,
You cannot persuade me it's a crime
If they make love while they still have time,
But you who for learning have no rival,
Tell us the teachings of the Bible;
Where are we taught to pervert our senses
And make our natural needs offences?
To fly from lust as in Saint Paul
Doesn't mean flight from life and all,
But to leave home and friends behind
And stick to one who pleased one's mind.

160

But I'm at it again! I'll keep my place;
It isn't for me to judge the case,
When you, a spirit born and queen
Remember the texts and what they mean,
With apt quotations well-supplied
From the prophets who took the woman's side,
And the words of Christ that were never belied
Who chose for His Mother an earthly bride.

"But oye, what use are pishrogue and spell
To one like myself in the fires of Hell?
What chance can there be for girls like me
With husbands for only one in three?
When there's famine abroad the need advises
To look after yourself as chance arises,
And since crops are thin and weeds are plenty,
And the young without heart and Ireland empty,
And to fill it again is a hopeless job,
Get me some old fellow to sit by the hob;
Tie him down there as best you can—
And leave it to me to make him a man."

4

The day crept in and the lights grew pale,
The girl sat down as she ended her tale;
The princess rose with face aglow
And her voice when she spoke was grave and slow.
"Oyez!" said the clerk to quell the riot,
And wielded his mace till all were quiet,
Then from her lips as we sat hushed
Speech like a rainbow glory gushed.
"My child," she said, "I will not deny
That you've reason enough to scold and cry,
And, as a woman, I can't but grieve

161

To see girls like you, and Moll and Maeve,
With your dues diminished and favours gone,
And none to enjoy a likely man
But misers sucking a lonely bone
Or hairy old harpies living alone.
I do enact according then
That all the present unmarried men
Shall be arrested by the guard,
Detained inside the chapel yard
And stripped and tied beside the gate
Until you decide upon their fate.
Those that you find whom the years have thwarted
With masculine parts that were never exerted
To the palpable loss of some woman's employment,
The thrill of the milk and their own enjoyment;
Who, having the chance of wife and home
Went wild and took to the hills to roam,
Are only a burden on the earth
So give it to them for all you're worth.
Roast or pickle them, some reflection
Will frame a suitable correction,
But this you can choose at your own tribunal,
And whatever you do will have my approval.
Fully grown men too old to function
As I say you can punish without compunction;
Nothing you do can have consequences
For middle-aged men with failing senses,
And, whatever is lost or whatever survives,
We need never suppose will affect their wives—
Young men, of course, are another affair;
They still are of use, so strike with care!

"There are poor men working in rain and sleet,
Out of their minds with the troubles they meet,

162

But, men in name and in deed according,
They quarry their women at night and morning—
A fine traditional consolation!—
And these I would keep in circulation.
In the matter of priests a change is due,
And I think I may say it's coming, too.
Any day now it may be revealed
That the cardinals have it signed and sealed,
And we'll hear no more of the ban on marriage
Before the priests go entirely savage.
Then the cry of the blood in the body's fire
You can quicken or quell to your heart's desire,
But anyone else of woman born,
Flay him alive if he won't reform!
Abolish wherever my judgment reaches
The nancy boy and the flapper in breeches,
And when their rule is utterly ended
We can see the world that the Lord intended.

"The rest of the work must only wait.
I'm due elsewhere and already late;
I've business afoot that I must attend
Though you and I are far from the end,
For I'll sit next month and God help the men
If they haven't improved their ways by then!
But mostly those who sin from pride
With women whose names they do not hide,
Who keep their tally of ruined lives
In whispers, nudges, winks and gibes.
Was ever vanity more misplaced
Than in married women and girls disgraced?
It isn't desire that gives the thrust,
The smoking blood and the ache of lust,
Weakness of love and the body's blindness

But to punish the fools who show them kindness.
Thousands are born without a name
That braggarts may boast of their mothers' shame—
Men lost to Nature through conceit,
And their manhood killed by their own deceit,
For 'tis sure that however their wives may weep
It's never because they go short of sleep."

I'd listened to every word she uttered,
And then as she stopped my midriff fluttered;
I was took with a sort of sudden reeling
Till my feet seemed resting on the ceiling;
People and place went round and round,
And her words came back as a blur of sound.
Then the bailiff strode along the aisle
And reached for me with an ugly smile;
She nipped my ear as if in sport
And dragged me up before the court.
Then the girl who'd complained of how she was slighted,
Spotted my face and sprang up, excited.
"Is it you?" says she. "Of all the old crocks!
I'm waiting for years to comb your locks.
You had your chance and you missed your shot,
And devil's cure to you now you're caught!
Will anyone here speak in your favour
Or even think you worth the labour?
What little affair would you care to mention
Or what girl did you honour with your attention?
We'll all agree that the man's no beauty,
But, damn it, he's clearly fit for duty.
I know, he's ill-made and ugly as hell,
But he'd match some poor misfortunate well.
I'd sooner him pale and not quite so fat,
But the hump's no harm; I'd make nothing of that

For it isn't a thing you'd notice much
Or one that goes with the puritan touch.
You'll find bandy legs on men of vigour
And arms like pegs on a frolicsome figure.
Of course there must be some shameful reason
That kept him single out of season.
He's welcome at the country houses,
And at the villagers' carouses,
Called in wherever the fun is going,
And fiddles being tuned and whiskey flowing—
I'll never believe there's truth in a name:
A wonder the Merrymans stand the shame!
The doggedest devil that tramps the hill
With grey in his hair and a virgin still!
Leave me alone to settle the savage!
You can spare your breath to cool your porridge!
The truth of it's plain upon your forehead;
You're thirty at least and still unmarried!
Listen to me, O Fount of Luck,
This fellow's the worst that ever I struck.
All the spite I have locked inside
Won't let me at peace till I've tanned his hide.
Can't ye all help me? Catch him! Mind him!
Winnie, girl, run and get ropes to bind him!
Where are you, Annie, or are you blind?
Sally, tie up his hands behind!
Molly and Maeve, you fools what ails you?
Isn't it soon the courage fails you?
Hand me the rope till I give him a crack;
I'll earth it up in the small of his back.
That, young man, is the place to hurt you;
I'll teach you to respect your virtue!
Steady now, till we give him a sample!
Women alive, he's a grand example!

Set to it now and we'll nourish him well!
One good clout and ye'll hear him yell!
Tan him the more the more he'll yell
Till we teach his friends good manners as well.
And as this is the law to restore the nation
We'll write the date as a great occasion—
'The First of January, Seventeen Eighty—' "

And while I stood there, stripped and crazy,
Knowing that nothing could save my skin,
She opened her book, immersed her pen,
And wrote it down with careful art,
As the girls all sighed for the fun to start.
And then I shivered and gave a shake,
Opened my eyes, and was wide awake.

Bryan Merryman (? –1805)

Endpiece

An end to all I've ever had to say,
An end to all the golden girls and gay,
An end, thank God, to sorrow's feverish sway—
And Christ be with me on the Judgment Day.